FOR LOVE AND MONEY

EXPLORING SEXUAL & FINANCIAL BETRAYAL IN RELATIONSHIP

By Debra L. Kaplan

For Information Contact:

Debra L. Kaplan
MBA, MA, LPC, CMAT, CSAT-S
6151 E. Grant Road
Tucson, Arizona 85712
(520) 203-1943

www.debrakaplancounseling.com
email: info@debrakaplancounseling.com

To
Vicki, Vi, Ing
and their Montys

ADVANCE PRAISE

"**W**ith wit and compassion, Debra Kaplan explores how early relational trauma greatly disturbs a person's ability to be honest and mature in relationship around issues of power, sex and money. An excellent read!"

-**Pia Mellody** author of *Facing Codependence*, *Facing Love Addiction* and *Breaking Free*. Also a co-author with Larry Freundlich of *The Intimacy Factor*

"Love, money, sex, the quest for power, and the need for attachment - Debra Kaplan combines state of the art research, a wealth of clinical wisdom, and insights drawn from her own life to provide a deep and searing light into not only each of these, but, most brilliantly, the way they commonly interact in our closest, most cherished and most painful relationships. Illuminating the secret dynamics of control, submission, and betrayal, *For Love and Money*, is one of the most fearless, honest explorations of the intricacies of relationships that you are ever likely to encounter. More than explanation, it offers a practical guide for healing. It gripped me from the first page. Readable, compelling, and important - it has the power to change your life."

-**Terry Real**, author of New Rules of Marriage & I Don't Want to Talk About It

"Debra Kaplan is an author who possesses a unique skill set: She spent many years in the financial world as a successful Wall Street trader, after which she became a nationally recognized psychotherapist specializing in trauma and sex addiction. The result is a thought-provoking unusual book that melds these two worlds as she addresses the challenges of clients whose dysfunctional and self-destructive behaviors involve *both* sex and money. Providing many examples, *For Love and Money* explores the childhood roots of these behaviors, money as an aphrodisiac, the role of power and control, and "financial infidelity" among other relevant topics—and also how both clients and their spouses can be helped. It will be an eye-opener for many readers. I highly recommend it."

-Jennifer Schneider, M.D. Ph.D., author of *Disclosing Secrets: An Addict's Guide for When, to Whom, and How Much to Reveal*

"In *For Love and Money*, Debra Kaplan expertly weaves together sound research and insightful clinical observations that disentangle the complex dynamics that link sex, money, and power in relationships. Shedding light on the darkness that surrounds money and sexual secrets that violate the fabric of trust, *For Love and Money* is certain to be a book that contributes to our understanding of what heals sexual and financial betrayal."

-Kenneth M. Adams, Ph.D., CSAT-S, author of *Silently Seduced, When Parents Make Their Children Partners* and *When He's Married to Mom*

"*For Love and Money* brilliantly explores the volatile and exploitive world where addiction is fused with money, finance and relationships. Kaplan's unique background as a former Wall Street trader turned therapist and educator makes her the perfect person to guide the reader on an illuminating journey into the jaws of sexual exploitation, aggressive power tactics, money obsession, eroticized rage, and relational power. This riveting and timely page turner will be sure to leave the reader hungry for more."

- Stefanie Carnes, PhD, LMFT, author of *Mending A Shattered Heart: A Guide for Partners of Sex Addicts* and *Facing Heartbreak: Steps to Recovery for Partners of Sex Addicts*

"Debra Kaplan takes her insight and passion from her journey from the world of finance and power to the solitude of the therapist's chair. Using real-life clinical examples she follows the conscious, unconscious and societal quest for "more" which fuels marginalization, discrimination and abuse. Kaplan explores the sexual, spiritual and relational dissatisfaction that often fuels financial exploitation. Using the vulnerability of her own journey and speaking clearly in her own voice, Kaplan's unique perspective explores the psychological development of attachment and human disconnection. Finally, she addresses resolution through a healing journey to communication and restoration within the individual and in relationships."

-Jes Montgomery, MD., Psychiatric Director, Sex Addiction Treatment Program at Pine Grove Behavioral Health

"The use of money to express rage and dominate human life is part of our everyday discussion. But when this dynamic manifests in our intimate relationships, we become silent. Deb Kaplan boldly elucidates how money is used as a form of violence and domination and exchanged for sex in intimate partnerships and family systems. Her concept of "monetized rage" is both brilliant and so necessary for any psychotherapist today."

-Omar Minwalla, Psy.D., The Institute for Sexual Health (ISH)

"For Love and Money is amazing. This book needs to be out there for the general public and it's a "must-read" for clinicians as well."

-Rokelle Lerner, Clinical Director of InnerPath Retreats for Cottonwood Tucson, author of *The Object of My Affection is in My Reflection: Coping with Narcissists*

ACKNOWLEDGEMENTS

I wish to acknowledge several key people for their contribution to this book.

I want to thank Jennifer Schneider for her unwavering guidance and constructive feedback throughout the evolution of this book. Jennifer's literary and editorial acumen, as well as close friendship, was instrumental in the direction and flow of *For Love and Money*. For that and so much more, *thank you, Jennifer!*

I wish to acknowledge Scott Brassart. He took the chapters and turned them into a book worth reading. But most importantly he took this project (me) from a near fatal implosion and steered it (me) to its (my) resurrection. *Thank you, Scott!*

I owe a debt of gratitude to Bonnie DenDooven. She is my friend, colleague and champion and it is on her shoulders that I stand tall. Her generous desire to share her knowledge with me remains an inspiration and for that I am sincerely appreciative.

I owe a deep personal and professional debt of gratitude to Dr. Patrick Carnes. It is because of his vision and courage that the field of sex addiction weighs as prominently as it does today. And it was on the merit of his personal insight almost fourteen years ago that I set forth on my own not-so-gentle path of recovery. Years later he has entrusted me with his confidence to expand on his vision and I am grateful. I hope that *For Love and Money* has delivered on that faith.

No one person wished for this book to be finished more than my partner Lance. He remained a strong champion in spite of my physical and emotional absence. His support began in Cabo San Lucas and lasted up until the end. *Thank you, Lance. I know it wasn't easy.*

Last, I would like to acknowledge my sons. Your persistent question of, "Is it done yet?" served as a familiar echo of yesteryear and a battle cry to the finish line. I am proud to be your mom and even prouder that you are my sons. Your collective brilliance, humor and sensitivity remain so dear to my heart. So, Lance, Jared and Jonah; *It's done!*

CONTENTS

AUTHOR'S NOTE

For years I have served my clients in a variety of widely diverse therapeutic settings. These have included hospital psychiatric units, first responder crisis and de-escalation emergency services; residential treatment, workshops and intensives; and individual office settings. In these venues I have worked with doctors, clergy, national security and high-ranking military personnel, financiers, attorneys, and students, to name just a few. In all settings I maintain a staunch commitment to confidentiality in my work. As such, all individuals, couples, circumstances, and narratives presented in these pages are fictionalized and composite in nature. All names and case histories are conceptual adaptations altered by gender, name, circumstance, and therapeutic struggle in order to represent an illustrative example while also protecting patient anonymity. If any person or situation in the book bears a resemblance to a specific person or circumstance in life this is entirely coincidental. Stories depicting financial and political historical events are real, though occasionally condensed for brevity and relevance.

FOREWORD

In today's America our individual and cultural focus on financial success and the outward trappings that money can bring has left a void of cultural understanding about what it takes to experience innate joy via community and genuine intimacy. Without using the standard labels and judgments often applied to those who succeed financially yet remain emotionally empty, *For Love and Money* looks closely at those who search for ever more "stuff" in a vain attempt to alleviate the pain of childhood trauma and poor parenting. Throughout the book, readers can see how the drive for financial success, power, control, and sexual conquest can lead some people to not only a figurative but also a literal downfall. The harder they work and the more they have the less they feel alive, connected, and part-of, and the worse their lives get. It is only through great effort and sacrifice that these individuals are able to overcome the adult difficulties they were programmed for in childhood. Men and women, who are willing to do the work of healing, are uniformly and deeply grateful for the journey once the road of recovery has been traveled.

In *For Love and Money*, author Debra Kaplan challenges all of us to look into the delicate interplay of early childhood experience and adult behavioral and emotional dysfunction. This book helps explain both how and why a person might consistently, albeit unconsciously, value financial status, sexual prowess and shiny objects over intimacy, family, and genuine emotional intimacy. More than a simplistic view of narcissism and self-obsession, her words offer a much needed, compassionate, and perceptive look into the world of intelligent, well-educated, and successful men and women who somehow make empty, seemingly meaningless choices when it comes to personal relationships, life priorities, and the way they define meaning and self-worth. Debra's wealth of experience in both the financial and clinical worlds allows us a unique view into the issues faced by those who have so much externally, yet find themselves starved for meaning and connection. *For Love and Money* opens with an examination of how our childhoods affect our adulthoods, along with a brief and cogent review of attachment styles. Readers are offered meaningful insight into the ways that early life experiences affect adult bonding and relationship choices. The book also walks us through the ways in which unresolved childhood trauma (emotional, physical, and/or sexual) and its resulting adult low self-esteem and shame can later manifest in maladaptive coping mechanisms. In an important nod to the challenges of living today, Debra is succinctly focused here on the frequently empty (yet emotionally arousing) obsessive search for money, power, status, and sexual conquest. These understandings are the underpinning of all that follows in the book, and they are cleverly couched in the language and content of the very clients she has been treating.

In many ways the author's approach to this material mirrors my own work, though Debra applies the information to a somewhat different arena of adult life. We both focus on sexual disorders, primarily sex and intimacy addictions, but Debra's focus also encompasses the areas of financial control, manipulation, and exploitation in sexual and intimate relationships. And it will probably come as no surprise to readers to learn that money and sex are rather thoroughly intertwined in many instances as the issues that underlie them—depression, anxiety, unresolved trauma, attachment deficit disorders, and the like—often have similar expressions in adult life. Simply put, Debra and I each see in our practices a wide variety of men and women who have learned to deal with early trauma, life stressors, and underlying psychological conditions by "numbing out" with obsessive, adrenaline-rush-inducing thoughts and behaviors—be it the high of closing a high-stakes deal, the excitement of a new sexual conquest, the power of controlling a spouse or partner via money or sex, or some combination thereof.

The book next provides an examination of how these types of relationships are formed and maintained, focusing primarily on how money and sex affect power and control in intimate relationships. The author delves into topics like the ways in which money (who earns how much, who spends how much, and why) can become the chief source of strife, blame, and judgment in relationships, even though finances are in reality merely the symbol/symptom of deeper relational issues. When couples are fighting about money, they are more likely fighting about power, control, fear of abandonment, emotional distance, and other issues that cause the unconscious perception of repeated childhood trauma. In other words, one or both parties are reminded of the pain and angst experienced in childhood as the result of inadequate parenting, trauma, etc.

Happily, as mentioned above, the book looks at the many similarities of sexual and financial infidelity, along with the fact that they often occur in tandem. Think, for instance, about the high-level male executive with an ongoing extramarital affair. Usually he is not just cheating sexually, but financially, as he pays his mistress's rent and other bills, buys her lavish gifts, etc., all without his wife's knowledge let alone consent. Sometimes a man (occasionally a woman) cheats in this or similar ways to the point where he (or she) does real and lasting damage to not only his (or her) primary relationship, but his (or her) family's finances. Yet even on the verge of bankruptcy the problematic behaviors continue. Unfortunately, many clients get help only after the negative consequences of their financial and sexual shenanigans are so severe they can no longer be ignored.

And the pain experienced by these individuals, not to mention the pain experienced by their spouses, is quite literally palpable. This is what clinicians everywhere deal with on a regular basis, and Debra does a wonderful job of presenting the manifestations of this very real hurt, loss, and humiliation. All the while she reminds us that it is the emotional scarcity learned in childhood—leading to adult desperation in financial/sexual matters—that fosters the pain-inducing adult choices that healthier individuals simply would not make.

Most importantly, the reader is not left hanging with a mere explanation of the problems faced by so many individuals and couples today. Debra uses the final third of the book to walk us back from the brink, providing clear and concise explanations of the practices, principles, and tools inherent to healing, enabling readers to both live and love in happier, healthier ways. Of greatest value to the reader is the insight into the ways that early disruptions in emotional growth can affect adult financial and sexual choices. The reader is guided toward healing by illuminating what can be done to change the ways in which we think and act as adults, especially in regard to intimacy. Throughout the book the author provides us with real-world examples, telling the stories of real people (while protecting their identities) as a way to illustrate the academic points she makes. Almost anyone reading *For Love and Money* is likely to identify with at least a few of these tales, and to find comfort in the fact that others with similar problems have managed to find relief and build a better life. In this way, the examples—the stories of healing and growth away from objectified experiences and toward genuine joy, fun, and creativity—are not only enlightening but inspiring.

Realistically, the author recognizes that there is no magic bullet that will automatically cure the ills of people who have long-term histories of acting out with sex and money. Debra accurately notes that healing is a lengthy and arduous process involving individual and group therapy, external support groups, twelve-step recovery, and numerous forms of self-education and enlightenment (perhaps with this book as a meaningful start). Along the way many difficult questions must be asked, examined, and ultimately answered. For most, the healing process is sometimes fun, sometimes frightening, sometimes mortifying, but it is always worth the effort.

Robert Weiss LCSW, CSAT-S

Robert Weiss is the author of *Cruise Control: Understanding Sex Addiction in Gay Men* and *Sex Addiction 101: A Basic Guide to Healing from Sex, Love, and Porn Addiction*, and co-author with Dr. Jennifer Schneider of both *Untangling the Web: Sex, Porn, and Fantasy Obsession in the Internet Age* and *Closer Together, Further Apart: The Effect of Technology and the Internet on Sex, Intimacy and Relationships*.

PREFACE

I am often asked how I went from Wall Street commodity option trader to trauma and sex addiction therapist. The leap might sound rather incongruous, but in reality it was natural.

I began my career in business in the early 1980s trading physical commodities.1 As freighters made their way around the globe and before their arrival in the U.S., I arranged distribution of the expected commodity via barge and ship, up and down our country's inland waterways. My job was to oversee the offload and delivery of bulk commodities such as Nitrogen, Phosphorus and Potassium, after freighters arrived at their port of call (in New Orleans or North Carolina, for example). Overseeing an offload involved standing on the pier—hard hat and all -- followed by a courtesy drink with the tanker's captain. The hard hat was clearly mandatory; the drink was clearly not! Those early years taught me a lot about how physical commodities were traded and transported, but I also learned that addictions are rampant in the shipping industry. Drinking and driving cars? That's nothing compared to drinking and piloting ships and barges.

In the mid-1980s I took a position with a large Wall Street brokerage firm to market and sell high-yield bonds. From 1981 through late 1982 the U.S. experienced a gripping recession that was followed by a powerful bull market. That bull market was fueled by low interest rates, hostile corporate takeovers, and leveraged buyouts. In a leveraged buyout, a company is purchased with a combination of equity, plus significant (operative word here being *significant*) amounts of borrowed money. So, where did this borrowed money come from? It was raised by selling high-yield bonds or junk bonds because of their non-investment grade rating yet risky investment appeal. To better understand the economic environment one need only think of novelist Tom Wolfe's fictional bond trader, Sherman McCoy, in *Bonfire of the Vanities* or Oliver Stone's fictional character and main antagonist, Gordon Gekko, of the 1987 film *Wall Street.*

The late 80s saw the meteoric rise in corporate raiders2, fueled by junk bonds and a raider's ability to exploit the financial vulnerability of the acquired company. The purchases were often hostile takeovers and resulted in the dismantling of operations or assets of the newly acquired company. Along with the takeovers on Wall Street came the hubris of indulgence. If we're speaking about "Masters of the Universe" then we would need to include bond traders in their epochal glory. Every bond guy (and the rare woman like myself) knew the buy and sell price of bonds, but more importantly we knew the buy and sell price of a person. As we saw it, everyone could be bought; the only real question was at what price. Sex and money might as well have been traded as their own commodities on Wall Street—forget about trading financial assets. Those ensuing years brought increasing concerns about the seemingly unstoppable and rampant economic spending and debting. That concern materialized when the stock market lost 22.6% of its value or $500 billion dollars on October 19, 1987.

Two days after the stock market crashed I stepped out of the elevator of One World Trade Center (the North Tower) to interview for a new position with a company called Cantor Fitzgerald in their Treasury bond market. As I peered down from the 103rd floor of One World Trade Center, looking out over the Hudson River, I thought, "*What the fuck do you do up here in a fire? 'cause you're not getting out.*" By the conclusion of the interview, just after I was offered the position, I instinctively knew that this job was not what I wanted, so I respectfully declined the offer and closed the meeting. I realized that I wanted to trade commodities one hundred floors below in Wall Street's adrenaline-fueled trading pits rather than in an ivory tower.3 On Sept. 11, 2001 the unforeseen deaths of thousands in the North and South Towers were heading for the history books and Cantor Fitzgerald suffered the greatest loss of life of any company that day. In 1987, I knew nothing about the terrorist attacks that were destined to demolish the towers and forever change the world as we knew it. But what I did know was to follow my gut and pursue an opportunity elsewhere on Wall Street almost one hundred floors below. It was not my time to die.

The world of floor trading gave new meaning to intensity — drug use, drinking, sexual hookups, affairs, sexual exploitation, control, power, and, addiction. Did I mention money? Adrenaline, sex, drugs, and money: What more could any addictive personality want? Traders are, by their nature, self-indulgent and prone to excess, and if excess and intensity were good, then *more* excess and intensity was better.

Gradually, however, I grew more fascinated with human behavior than I was with the markets. Or, should I say, I grew more fascinated by the behavior that drove the markets. I became captivated by the dynamics in the trading pit when fear took over or cold and calculating intensity switched on in the height of a trading frenzy.

Counter to what most people think, the markets do exhibit psychological states. In fact, in 2002 the Nobel Prize in Economics was awarded to two researchers for their work on human judgment and decision-making under uncertainty.4 The newly evolving field of neuroeconomics addresses this very phenomenon -- a combination of neuroscience, experimental and behavioral economics, and cognitive and social psychology. If there is one area to which the phrase *heady stuff* applies, it must be here! Add sexual and financial exploitation to the mix and we're really looking at a robust field of inquiry.

Eventually my interest in the personal dynamics related to money, sex, and relationship control – fueled by my own personal therapy – overtook my fascination with the marketplace and I changed careers, though I have never quite abandoned my interest in money, sex, and power. Hence this book – a fusion of my interests: money, sex, and the control they create – looking at how these things interrelate in real life, in real individuals, in real couples. Basically, what I have found in my 12 years as a therapist is that money, sex, and control are issues that have as much potency on Main Street as they do on Wall Street. The push/pull of these desires is inextricably snarled in the retelling of women and men's stories that I hear every day, especially when some form of addiction is present. And when that addiction is sex addiction, things get particularly interesting.

Nowadays, as a business woman turned therapist, working with individuals and couples in treatment is nothing less than invigorating and inspiring. And yet it is way more vexing than tiptoeing through the chaos and turmoil of the minefields of the financial markets. Covert and overt emotions influence the markets (especially in the commodity trading pits), and those same human emotions also drive our romantic needs, wants, and struggles. No surprises there. However, emotions in the financial realm are played out in a structure that has a beginning, middle, and end. The markets open and close, and a new trading day begins only after its predecessor finishes. Ultimately, the outcomes are tallied and finite. But relationships are not a zero-sum game. The outcomes cannot be measured, tallied, and quantified on a spreadsheet, with spoils to the winner.

I could not have become the therapist I am today had I not first been a client. At times I will reflect on my personal journey in this book because, as a therapist, I've done the hard work. I've walked through hell and reached the other side, a better person for the journey. And by working through my own struggles I have gained a personal perspective about change, as opposed to just an intellectual awareness. Of course, my clients' journeys are their own to take and each of them differs from my own; I am just honored to walk with them as they grow. That said, it is because of my own strength, hope, and courage that I remain committed to their change even when they themselves lose faith in the process.

I often tell them, "I'll have faith for the both of us until you can have faith for yourself."

While I was writing this book I called my own therapist, Vicki. I wanted her perspective about what she observed in me during my early days of treatment and recovery. I knew my journey from the inside looking out, but I wanted to know what she saw from the outside looking in. "What do you believe helped me the most?" I asked.

"Your heart wasn't open and mine was," Vicki said. "When you came to see me, I knew that you were smarter than me. There was no way I could meet you at your intellectual level, but I could mirror back to you my heart."

Her words couldn't have rung more true. I remember a session when Vicki guardedly suggested that perhaps I was defensive. *"Defensive? Seriously? I'm not defensive! Are you kidding me?"* Vicki had merely smirked at me and asked, "Need I say more?" That simple response said it all.

Ultimately, what therapy provided me was empathic support and simultaneous accountability for my behaviors. I desperately needed both right from the start, though I didn't realize it at the time, because it took many months for me to even acknowledge that my heart wasn't open and loving, and many more months to do something about it. When I showed up in Vicki's office for our first session I thought I was in a healthy marriage, but in hindsight I see clearly that I knew little, if anything at all, about how to be emotionally open. Not only did my well-being depend on change, but the emotional well-being of my two young boys was also dependent on it. They did not have a choice; I did.

Being open and vulnerable in my relationship did not come easy. My history drove my problematic behaviors, which were all about protection and invulnerability. This defense worked in business and on the trading floor; it didn't work nearly as well in my relationships or marriage. My work with Vicki taught me how to be relational by way of being open and accepting. In the process, it helped me to listen without defending, speak without contempt, and have compassion for myself and for others. At the time I was not grateful for the painful lessons I learned, but I am incredibly grateful now for the knowledge that I ultimately gleaned about myself in therapy.

Nowadays, because I have traveled the difficult path they are just starting, I am in awe of my clients' courage. In our therapeutic work together they risk everything, facing their fears, becoming vulnerable and allowing me to witness their struggles. It is an honor to walk with them on their journeys.

Because of this, I simply *had* to write *For Love and Money*. If you have ever found yourself in the crosshairs of sexual and financial control and exploitation, as I have, then this book is for you.

WHERE WE ARE GOING

Money for sex and sex for power can play out across many relationships, cultures, and demographics. There is no one socioeconomic stratum – be it profession, personality type, gender, ethnicity, sexual orientation, age, education level, or any other identity – that has cornered the market on exploitation. The battle for power and control by way of sex and money is universal. We can see it (albeit to a small degree) even in most healthy relationships. And in unhealthy relationships it can become an all-consuming driving force toward misery and destruction.

This thorny phenomenon, which I first observed on Wall Street, is intriguing to observe and treat as a therapist, though sometimes downright disconcerting. And, although much has been written about finances, and much has been written about sex, very little has been written about the ways in which finances and sex often intersect to create power and control in relationships.

Many, but not all, of the case studies included in this book involve sex addicts. In my practice I work with complex trauma, attachment, and sex addiction. Those who exploit or are exploited by sex and money in relationships are not always sex addicts, but I do find that most sex addicts in relationships tend to use sex and money as weapons of control. Sexual compulsivity at its core is a disease of the self-absorbed, and so is exploitation. Thus these two phenomena often travel hand-in-hand. You don't have to be a sex addict (or involved with a sex addict) to experience the dynamics of sexual and financial betrayal to benefit from reading this book. Whether or not addiction is a part of your struggle, it is my belief that you will benefit nonetheless from understanding the dynamics of power and control because relationships are oftentimes about that. How we learn to handle compromise and influence is pertinent to all relationships across all demographics.

Whether you are the person being exploited or the one doing the exploiting, insight will be mandatory for change. Given this, I've included tools and exercises at the end of each chapter that are designed to help *either partner* begin the process of introspection and growth. I have opted for exercises beneficial to both partners because if you are on the receiving end in an exploitive relationship and your partner, the person doing the exploiting, is not willing to change, you will need to manifest change within yourself. As therapists often say, "maintaining our own side of the street" is essential to growth and recovery. Furthermore, the balance of power in a relationship can shift if just one person, whether exploiter or exploited, modifies their behavior. Moving toward developing healthy relationships first with yourself and by association with your partner may be what jumpstarts the new relational order. Developing a new relationship with ourselves, our partners, our money, and our sexual enjoyment takes work from both sides of the partnership, and it starts with you!

Part One of the book, "Sex, Love, and Longing," explores bonding and attachment from a biopsychosocial perspective. The goal here is to understand our primal brain and how, as adults, our past traumas influence who we attract and to whom we are attracted. This section also looks at how early unresolved trauma and shame often create a maladaptive need for external power and control, which may well be achieved through exploitation of sex and/or money.

Part Two of the book, "Sex, Money, and Power," builds on the concepts explored in Part One by further shaping the addictive and overarching foundation on which relationships are built, focusing particularly on the power and control dynamic and the inherent roles of sex and money.

Part Three of the book, "Back from the Brink," describes the distinct practices, principles, and tools that are inherent in a healthy relationship, teaching a healthier approach to monetary, sexual, and psychological wellbeing. Ideas, tools, and exercises are provided, giving guidance for self-empowerment and relational balance. At the close of each chapter I've provided questions to answer about yourself and your partner.

Please note that *For Love and Money* does not address the problems that arise when a relationship has to cope with financial stressors. Those problems can range from having a minor impact on the relationship all the way to severe discord or divorce. As you will see many studies rank money concerns as the most frequent issue for arguments. However, the subject of "insufficient funds" is important and merits attention; a direction, perhaps, for another book.

It is my sincere hope that by the end of this book you will have a better understanding of how your past traumas affect your present relationship decisions, for better and worse, as well as what you can do to change the dynamics of your relationship if it is not working as well as you would like. And, let's face it, you wouldn't be reading this book if it were! Good luck to you.

PART I:

SEX, LOVE, AND LONGING

We are like children building a sand castle. We embellish it with beautiful shells, bits of driftwood, and pieces of colored glass. The castle is ours, off limits to others. We're willing to attack if others threaten to hurt it. Yet despite all our attachment, we know that the tide will inevitably come in and sweep the sand castle away. The trick is to enjoy it fully but without clinging, and when the time comes, let it dissolve back into the sea.

— *Pema Chödrön*

Adam paused before answering my question about what he'd done as a child to get approval. His eyes squinted sideways and his gaze wandered off beyond my office window, his mind floating to a time and place many years earlier. I watched as his facial expression changed to sullen, his left foot rhythmically displaying his agitation. And then, suddenly, "I did whatever I could to get noticed, basically. My father rarely had time for us because he was the President and CEO of a large manufacturing company, or *firm,* as he called it." Adam underscored his ire with air quotes as he spoke the word *firm.* "My mother drank. A lot. By the time I got to high school her drinking was really bad. When I came home from school in the afternoons she was usually passed out on the couch."

Adam was a good-looking man with chiseled facial features, and he stood straight despite his well above average height. (He described himself as pleasing enough in appearance, but lanky.) Although his eyes were seldom still, darting anxiously, scanning for whatever might be lurking out of view, he had an air of calm. When he smiled it was warm and inviting, but his smiles were rare and sporadic. By the time he was in his 30s, his anxiety overwhelmed him, especially if he went out on a date with or even had interest in a woman. His current relationship was turning serious, and this had raised his anxiety level to unbearable. That was when he decided to come in for therapy.

Adam had already told me that his family was well off financially, yet he'd come to resent money and all that it meant. "My father was a very rich man. He was able to buy anything for us. I guess that is how he showed his love, but what I really wanted more than anything was to be with him and spend time together. But he didn't even have time for my mother, let alone my three sisters and me."

Vietnamese Zen Buddhist monk Thich Nhat Hanh wrote in *True Love: A Practice for Awakening the Heart* that the most precious gift you can give someone is your true presence, and money can be an obstacle to that. "Being rich is an obstacle to loving," he said. "When you are rich, you want to continue to be rich, and so you end up devoting all your time, all your energy in your daily life, to staying rich." This is a lesson Adam learned early in life. The isolation and neglect he experienced as a boy affected the man he'd become. It was clear to me if not to Adam from where his resentment stemmed.

Adam came to resent his family's money because his feelings of loneliness endured throughout his life. In his family, his parents gave material goods in lieu of actively showing and sharing affection. Had Adam's father and mother been able or willing to really give of themselves and actively love him, he might have experienced and known a deep, secure familial intimacy. Instead he grew up with a sense of longing and a fear of people who were close to him. Of course, when he arrived in therapy he hadn't yet verbalized what money symbolized for him. All he knew was that he feared both being engulfed and being abandoned – two seemingly conflicting feelings. So the dilemma of wanting to be in a relationship yet fearing the very same thing plagued him. According to Adam, his only fleeting solace from this deeply entrenched anxiety was provided by obsessively counting and recounting his money, coupled with impulsive buying and spending. In Adam's case the past remained present. His anxiety was the result of his unresolved childhood trauma stemming from neglect by his father (and to a lesser extent his mother). For Adam, adult romantic relationships inevitably summoned his childhood pain.

For most of us, including Adam, the ways in which we experience distress in relationships stem largely from the type of family bonding (or outright trauma or abuse) we experienced in childhood. The duration of those traumatic occurrences and the family system in which we lived strongly influence how we experience connection as adults. Therefore, of substantial importance to secure connections in our adult relationships is the support system available to us in childhood, along with our own character traits, personality, and adaptability.

Further along in our sessions Adam was able to dispel the notion that his relationship was the root cause for his anxiety. "I know that my anxiety began when I started my relationship," he said, "but blaming the relationship or my girlfriend would be so cliché, no? We met online and we began this long and slow process of getting to know each other. I already knew that I get really anxious in a relationship, so I wasn't going to jump into anything too quickly."

I told Adam I was glad that he'd decided to take his time, given his past experiences.

He continued, saying, "Now that I have what I've always wanted – a loving relationship – I want out. I'm suffocating and my girlfriend is making demands of me, demands that I'm not prepared to meet."

"I completely understand," I said.

"So when she starts pushing too hard for a major commitment from me, I run. I disappear into porn and searching chat rooms."

Eventually Adam discovered that his fear of being emotionally vulnerable and therefore potentially hurt was at the heart of his relationship struggle(s). At that point, I hadn't even broached the likely equally distressing topic of money, mostly because I thought it was better, in Adam's case, to handle one minefield at a time. Whether Adam would be willing to open up his bank coffers (wealthy as they were) and share expenses with his girlfriend remained to be seen, but at least he'd finally made that first giant realization and come to understand that his fear of being vulnerable would have to be dealt with if he was ever going to find relationship happiness. Otherwise, his longing for sex and love would forever create more anxiety than fulfillment.

I'm often asked in therapy (with deep reluctance and trepidation, I might add) if it's a pre-requisite of therapy to explore childhood issues. "That depends," I say. "I have no desire to dwell on your past, but I certainly believe that revisiting or exploring your childhood relationships and traumas might help us both understand your current relationships and how you have come to view the world and the way in which you relate to it."

This is exactly what I told Adam the day he first came to understand that his relationship was not the underlying cause of his anxiety, merely the catalyst that set it in motion. Adam was correct when he acknowledged that blaming someone or something would be a quick and easy (as well as misguided) answer. Nevertheless, their dynamic was misaligned and fraught with angst. But the issues weren't so much with his girlfriend as they were with Adam himself. He was projecting his own fears onto his girlfriend and they were reflected back on himself, creating extreme anxiety.

EVEN THE LONGEST JOURNEY MUST BEGIN WHERE YOU STAND

I understood Adam's dilemma fully. My own personal unwillingness, or more aptly stated, my own inability to be emotionally available was something I'd never even thought about before I sought therapy and made a commitment for enduring change. The reason was simple: Growing up, I learned by experience that my emotional needs would not be met unless I took care of them myself. I learned to be self-sufficient, counter-dependent (meaning having no needs or wants), and above all avoidant. I didn't even know that I was emotionally unavailable, nor did I know even *how to be present* for myself, much less for a partner. And what I did not know didn't pose a problem for me – or so I thought. In fact, had my partner brought this to my attention, I would not have understood the concept. Of course, once in recovery I realized that I knew nothing about introspection or about asking the proverbial life questions: What do I need? How do I ask for what I need? What does it take to be emotionally available? Etc. Consequently, I had no idea of what I needed or how to ask for it. Emotionally present? What was that? Thus my relationship, like Adam's, was fraught with angst and fear – so much so that those negative emotions overrode the possibility of comfort and connection.

Over time I came to realize that my own inability to feel my emotions had an array of consequences for me and my family. I might have been present in my body and with my thoughts, but was I emotionally available to myself and to others? Not so much. I lacked a clear emotional connection to both myself and others. Happily, as a result of being in recovery, I learned to distinguish intimacy from intensity, to connect my head with my heart, to feel my feelings – if not for me then at least for my boys. My maternal mantra had always been to raise two emotionally connected and sensitive young men, even though I myself was neither. Needless to say, the void left by my emotional disconnection was glaring, and my recovery and the resulting emotional epiphany couldn't have come a minute too soon.

A week after realizing that his relationship was not the true cause of his anxiety, Adam sat in my waiting room looking agitated and not too happy to see me. He appeared to be losing weight. When I asked, he stated his intention was to become fit, but I suspected otherwise, as his tall, lean build was anything but out of shape. It seemed more likely to me that anxiety had diminished his appetite. Clearly, on this day, Adam was not his usual confident self. He looked like he was struggling to remain erect in the waiting room chair, and his shirt was disheveled, almost sloppy – highly unusual for him.

"I'm not happy to see you," he said, and he was not the least bit apologetic about it. "Lately I'm not particularly happy to see anyone, let alone you."

"I understand," I said. "Yet you're here, and I applaud you for your willingness, despite your feelings, to show up." Up to that point our work together had been slow and painful, and at times he'd come precariously close to quitting. Had he done so I would have understood. On this day I felt that showing up even though he truly did not want to was significant. It showed that he was committed to his process and had recognized that, as painful as it had become for him, he was making slow but steady progress. For one thing, he was beginning to understand the causes of his anxiety and his perception of being simultaneously swallowed and abandoned by his girlfriend.

To this point, Adam had not gotten up from his seat in the waiting room, and he appeared apathetic and unmotivated to do so. Recognizing this, I too sat down in the waiting room. By now everyone else in the office was gone for the day so it didn't matter too much where we conducted our session. Plus, a change in venue offered both of us new eyes and a different perspective by which to experience each other. Despite the oddity in the setting, Adam was engaging. I was comfortable, and neither of us felt any particular need to move to my office.

That day my work with Adam finally took some much needed detours back to his family-of-origin. "I had a good life growing up," he said. "Yeah, my dad was too busy with work, and my mom drank, but I wasn't abused and I never went without anything. My childhood was nothing like the stories you read, you know? It wasn't traumatic or dramatic or violent or any of that stuff. I was loved, and I was given everything that money could buy. I had no problems in school or anywhere else, really."

One question seemed to shift Adam's utopian perspective: What did you do to gain your parent's approval?

"If I did a good job at school or got good grades at school my dad was happy. Other than that I didn't get much more from him because he was busy. But, my mother on the other hand – all I had to do was breathe and she fawned over me."

"Is that *really* what you remember? I asked." With Adam's admission about his mother I felt a wave of sadness because it was clear that all of his previous recollections about his mother were about her absence in his life, not her affection. Adam stared straight ahead and exhaled, as if someone pulled his plug and let out his air. By then he had taken his shoes off and put his feet up on another waiting room chair. He tried to hold back tears but his pain was too strong and he began to quietly sob.

"She wasn't there for me. I needed her to be but that isn't true – she wasn't!"

Adam's pain turned to anger and he continued,

"I suppose she loved me for who I was but she was too lost in her drinking to show me, let alone pay real attention to me."

With his brief anger, Adam tapped into the pain and loneliness that he had never previously voiced out loud to anyone. He permitted years of his suppressed anguish to be released if for only a brief time, but that was enough. Adam's truth about his childhood was now out – the genie was out of the bottle, and he could no longer lie to himself or to others about how he really felt.

"I know she must have loved me for who I was but it was only when I started dating that she began to pay much if *any* attention to me. However, it was the girls, not me that she fawned over. So I started feeling uncomfortable with the girls."

"Can you say more about that discomfort?"

"Yeah,"

His voice trailed off again and we sat in silence. His eyes became soft and teary.

"I guess I felt like I do now – suffocated and panicked. I felt claustrophic in a relationship even when there wasn't a problem. I wasn't able to speak to my girlfriends about it, like I'm doing with you now, but I guess, in a way I didn't like all the attention. I used to bail on the relationship and on my girlfriends."

"It sounds to me like all that attention is too much for you to handle. Adam, you said that you were feeling then, as you do now. What was it like to have a fawning mom – your description of your mom?"

"It was weird because I never felt like her attention was for or about me, and yet, it was. I felt crazy and ungrateful, and that's when it didn't feel so good. Like I said, she loved all the girls I dated so this isn't about my mom. My dad kept himself neck-deep in his work and money. He was not interested in getting me involved with his life unless it was to groom me for some business deal." Adam stopped talking and looked at me for a moment.

"You're probably going to tell me that I'm ungrateful for having such a good upbringing and that I'm really spoiled and just screwed up."

I assured him I had no intention of doing that. It was clear to me that as an adult, Adam's anxiety about his romantic relationships was deeply connected with his experiences of growing up with an absent mother and a distant father. But receiving adoration from his mother only when he became an adult and only after he was in a relationship was for Adam both problematic and a blessing. Had he not experienced any love or connection, he would not have had the ability to connect and therefore venture out into the world ready for intimate involvement as an adult.

However, his childhood disconnection with his mother and father did not offer him the significant understanding that he needed to recognize and tolerate difficult emotions that inevitably surface in romantic relationships. In his parents' marriage his father was distant and unable to talk about emotions. His mother's inconsistent and unreliable love and attention robbed him of his ability to feel secure in himself.

As an adult and in his romantic relationships Adam's unresolved issues quickly surfaced. His fearful avoidance became activated and emotional intimacy seemed more like a suffocating trap than a chosen loving connection. His unconscious fear of abandonment sent him running for sexual escape and the relational exit.

Starting that day in the waiting room, Adam's therapy sessions gradually helped him peel back the layers of his underlying distress and anxiety. Despite his reluctance to revisit his childhood, he instinctively realized from that time on that in order to go forward he had to first go back to the days when his current life behaviors regarding love, attachment, and connection were initially forged. Eventually he overcame the bulk of his fears and was able to move ahead with his existing relationship.

For Adam, his comfort and true emotional intimacy with his family of origin created his ongoing fears of loneliness, being abandoned, and potentially being exploited as an adult. His history with neglect and money as the substitute for love and attention led him to believe that romantic relationships occurred because of his financial worth rather than the love and connection he might bring to the equation. His fragile self-worth was established in childhood when he was given much in the way of material items and very little in the way of love and nurturing. He may have become financially rich, but he remained relationally poor.

As we will see throughout the remainder of this book, people accumulate objects of value to self-medicate or deflect their emotional insecurities. "Look at my worth, not at me!" For instance, Adam could go to his money and count it when he felt insecure. Unfortunately, that security had, for many years, kept him from seeking help with his true underlying issues, and thus his anxiety never went away (and in fact worsened over time). Before he came to therapy, he was self-medicating his symptoms without ever addressing his disease.

In the next chapter we'll explore the theory of attachment and the ways in which we learn to attach with our caregivers in childhood. As you read notice your own patterns in relationships and what style of attachment you most closely relate to.

CHAPTER 1

SEX, LOVE AND ATTACHMENT

In erotic love, two people who were separate become one. In motherly love, two people who were one become separate. The mother must not only tolerate, she must wish and support the child's separation.

— Erich Fromm

In romantic relationships there is both an interpsychic and an intrapsychic push/pull that occurs regarding our connections in the scope of emotional love, sexual longing, and ultimate desire. Interpsychic distress occurs *between* individuals, while intrapsychic distress occurs *within* an individual and is part of our internal process. As social and emotional creatures, we learn to negotiate our relationships with others from the earliest moments of being. Our earliest relationships with guardians and caregivers are how we learn to relate within ourselves and with/to others. At times the *intra* overcomes and/or clashes with the *inter.* When this happens in romantic relationships one person is emotionally zigging while the other is emotionally zagging, so to speak.

When one's *intra* is at odds with the other's *inter* (or vice versa) the results are at best painful and at worst tumultuous.

IN THE BEGINNING

(To the reader: for an in-depth understanding of attachment theory and the evolution in attachment research please see ***Addendum on Attachment***.)

The two names most synonymous with psychological attachment theory are John Bowlby and Mary D. Salter Ainsworth, and the brief discussion that follows is based heavily on their groundbreaking work.

Attachment is an emotional bond to another person. Bowlby, a British psychoanalyst, was the first to describe attachment as, "a lasting psychological connectedness between human beings."[1] He then developed what we now call "attachment theory" as an attempt to understand the intense distress experienced by infants when separated from their parents. According to Bowlby's theory, infants rely on caregivers, who become the child's perceived safe haven and eventual partner for emotional co-regulation. When the caregiver is emotionally healthy and available, an infant experiences comfort and learns to securely attach.

Bowlby further postulated that children are motivated by a primordial need to seek proximity and comfort from caregiver figures in times of distress, and that caregivers who are consistently available and responsive during times of distress are fundamental in creating a safe haven from which a child can explore the world and begin the process of safely and securely forming other attachments. He also delineated four key elements of attachment, shown below:

- Secure Base: A caregiver provides a consistent secure base from which the child can explore the world.

- Safe Haven: When in distress a child will return to the caregiver for comfort and soothing.

- Proximity Maintenance: The child attempts to stay near the caregiver, thus assuring safety.

- Separation Distress: When separated from the caregiver, a child will become upset and distressed.

Mary Ainsworth, an American-born psychologist, initially worked with John Bowlby, helping him to research maternal-infant attachments. She came to define attachment as an affectional tie that one person or animal forms between himself and another specific one – a tie that binds them together in space and endures over time.[2]

Later, Ainsworth worked on her own and eventually elaborated on Bowlby's findings and conclusions, creating an assessment tool to measure differences in attachments between mothers and their children. In particular, Ainsworth produced the now-famous "*Strange Situation*" study, in which a researcher observes a child's reactions when its mother briefly leaves the child alone in an unfamiliar room. The "*Strange Situation*" study led to Ainsworth's theory on attachment styles. Basically, she found three basic styles: Secure, Anxious-Ambivalent, and Anxious-Avoidant.

A child with a *Secure* attachment style becomes upset when his or her caregiver leaves and is soothed when the parent returns. When frightened, the child will seek proximity and closeness with the parent. In other words, the child embraces, accepts, and desires closeness given by the parent. A securely attached child may accept comfort from others; however, he continues to prefer a bonded parent.

Children with an *Anxious-Ambivalent* attachment style exhibit anxiety around strangers and new situations, even in the presence of his or her caregiver. The child's ambivalent attachment with the caregiver occurs after the caregiver departs (causing extreme distress for the child) and then returns. Upon the return of the parent the child will exhibit reluctance and anxiety in approaching the parent yet seeking and needing that closeness. This attachment style develops as a result of parenting which is disengaged, detached, or nonexistent. In these child/parent dynamics, the child's needs are ignored and unmet, and the child learns that attempts at connection will have no influence on the caregiver.

A child with an *Anxious-Avoidant* attachment style exhibits behavior that tends to ignore or turn away from the caregiver. While most children will seek closeness in the face of fear or uncertainty, a child with this attachment style shows little or no interaction with his or her caregiver. Psychologists believe that this is the result of a repeatedly disengaged and emotionally detached caregiver. As a result, a child will not prefer the parent over a stranger or show distress if the parent leaves.

TO LOVE OR BE LOVED: ADULT ATTACHMENT STYLES

Post-Bowlby and Ainsworth, researchers have studied the association between infant/childhood attachment styles and adult attachment styles, suggesting two primary conceptual dimensions in regard to adult attachment patterns: Avoidance (discomfort with closeness and/or dependency on others) and Anxiety (fear of rejection and abandonment).

Over time a measurement called the Experiences in Close Relationships (ECR) was developed, followed later by a revised version, commonly referred to as the ECR-R.[3] The ECR and ECR-R reflect a correlation between adult attachment styles and early childhood attachment styles. Researchers largely agree that a person's attachment style as an adult is shaped by his or her early interactions with parental attachment figures.[4] There are four basic adult attachment styles (as opposed to three for infants): Secure, Preoccupied, Fearful-Avoidant, and Dismissing-Avoidant (See Figure 1).

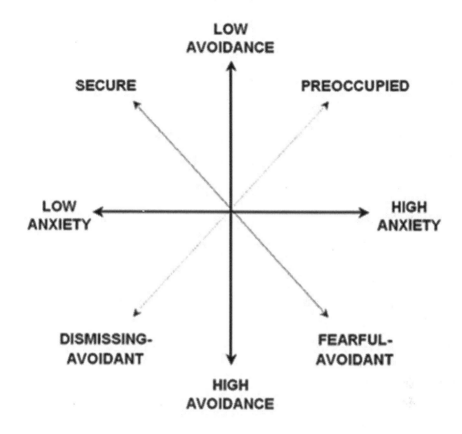

Figure 1. The two-dimensional model of individual differences in adult attachment.

The million dollar question, of course, is this: if early bonding and attachment are so vital to our later adult relationships, what happens to attachment in the face of not-good-enough parenting? In other words, how do the anxious and avoidant attachment patterns developed in infancy and childhood present in adult relationships? The answer is not likely to surprise you. For instance, in individuals like Adam – men and women who experience adult romantic relationships as anxiety provoking, uncomfortably enmeshing, and warranting escape – early childhood bonding and attachment to caregivers was, in all likelihood, either anxious-ambivalent or anxious-avoidant. Conversely, for people who find it easy to bond, connect with, and become emotionally intimate in adult romantic relationships, early childhood bonding and attachment was usually quite secure.

Essentially, where someone finds himself or herself on the anxiety and avoidance axis is indicative of the extent to which that person trusts and/or fears others in adult relationships. Likewise, where a person lands on the anxiety axis determines how safe or fearful that individual feels about being in relationship. Let's take a closer look.

SECURE ATTACHMENT STYLE (LOW ANXIETY, LOW AVOIDANCE)

- Nancy and Elliot are in love. They were friends for two years and dated for two more years before Elliot proposed. At first Elliot was hesitant about getting too involved with Nancy but his reluctance had less to do with Nancy and more to do with his previous relationship. A year earlier, Elliot had learned that his girlfriend was cheating on him with his best friend. Elliot always considered himself to be a trusting man, but this experience put his ease with women to the test. Nonetheless, when Elliot met Nancy he was smitten with her warmth and confidence. He also knew that he could not hold Nancy responsible for his previous girlfriend's actions. His ability to process and get past the pain, albeit at times with great anguish, was due to his solid self-esteem and ability to tolerate distressing emotions. For her part, Nancy was secure and did not become angry when at first Elliot had second thoughts about dating her. They both realized he needed time to heal, and they worked together to communicate their fear and concerns.

- Mary began online dating when she was 40 years old. After communicating and speaking with a few men she decided to meet one particular guy for coffee. While Mary did not know what the meeting would hold, and she was clear that her looks might not hold up under in-person scrutiny, she was secure in herself and confident enough to handle potential rejection.

- Geoff is an artist and was born with a speech impediment. He turned to drawing when he was young because he was shy and afraid of being ridiculed by children at school. His parents were aware of his insecurity and worked hard to show Geoff unconditional love and acceptance. As a teenager, Geoff was reluctant to date because of his speech impairment, but it didn't stop him from trying. Years later, Geoff became a successful artist and married his college sweetheart.

A person with a secure adult attachment style exhibits little to no anxiety or avoidance in relationship. Typically this individual also experienced secure attachment in infancy and childhood, having had a reliable caregiver who provided a safe haven and appropriate emotional co-regulation. Nancy, Mary, and Geoff all experienced a secure attachment style early on, and they are consequently able to mirror that in adulthood.

PREOCCUPIED ATTACHMENT STYLE (HIGH ANXIETY, LOW AVOIDANCE)

- Janet is obsessional about checking her partner's phone and laptop when he is in the shower. Although her partner has never been unfaithful or given her any reason to question his commitment to her or their relationship, she tends to be possessive. Janet often starts arguments just to convince herself that he isn't going to leave. While Janet wants his affection she is nonetheless afraid of getting too close. Her partner has begun to question if staying in the relationship is worth the struggle.

- Bryan knows that his wife is faithful, but he can't help but wonder why such a beautiful woman doesn't cheat on him. He often finds himself thinking, *"It is only a matter of time before she asks for a divorce and leaves me."*

- Gail was in several relationships before she met Jordon. Unlike her other boyfriends, Jordon stated that he would not sleep with other women. Despite Gail's concerns about Jordon's flirtation with women and his online sex chat behavior, she is afraid to leave. Over time his pornography use has increased, resulting in little to no sexual contact between them. Gail's anxiety has also increased, but she remains staunchly committed to staying with Jordon.

Consider Gail from the third example. Her ever-present distrust of Jordon has seriously compromised their relationship. And despite the sexual avoidance and emotional disconnect in the relationship she is unwilling to change the situation. A look back to Gail's childhood reveals that her mother was a doting mom to her three girls, despite her husband's ongoing infidelity. Furthermore, Gail's father worked long hours to make ends meet and was rarely physically or emotionally present with the family – except on weekends. It was then that Gail would accompany him on his fishing trips or jaunts to the local bar – anything just to be with him. She felt special when she was with him even though he spent the majority of his time joking with the others at the bar and laughing with the women who surrounded him. It never occurred to her that being with her dad meant doing only what he wanted and, worse yet, being emotionally abandoned and forced to watch the overt betrayal of her and the family.

The emptiness Gail felt growing up was minimally eased by those moments of being in her father's presence, despite the emotional distance. This early pattern of physical proximity with emotional distance carried into her adulthood. Her need for love, acceptance, and reassurance created a self-deprecating pattern of exploitation in her relationships, currently playing out in her lack of emotional (or even physical) bonding with Jordon.

When people with preoccupied attachment styles become overwhelmed by their fear and anxiety in the relationship they may use behaviors to ease their anxiety; such as compulsive or addictive processes to self-soothe their anxiety – alcohol, obsession with money, working, drugs, gambling, shopping, or sexual behavior.

This anxiety may also include picking fights to drive the other person away or becoming emotionally walled off and quiet. Regardless of the ways in which a person acts out their anxiety the result becomes a block to emotional closeness so as to minimize the pain if the relationship ends. Other times they simply end it, thinking "I'll hurt you before you can hurt me." However the anxiety manifests, the resultant behavior eventually pushes the partner away from the anxious individual. Over time this becomes a vicious and ever-worsening cycle.

FEARFUL-AVOIDANT ATTACHMENT STYLE (HIGH ANXIETY, HIGH AVOIDANCE)

- John is a 36-year old male who has yet to be in a romantic relationship. He is as fearful of women as he is fascinated by them, and wishes that he had the nerve to ask one out. He has worked for years in a large corporation, silently longing for several female coworkers. But instead of approaching them he goes home at night and lives out his fantasies in chat rooms and on porn websites.

- David and Ellen met online and were dating for four months when Ellen approached David seeking more emotional commitment from him. David became despondent and withdrew from the relationship, which became quite distressing for Ellen. After two weeks without any contact from David, Ellen arrived unannounced at his apartment to confront him. The only thing David said was, "I'm sorry that I am such a disappointment to you." He gave no explanation for his behavior.

- Judy spent many years in therapy hoping to heal from the wounds of childhood sexual and physical abuse. She believes most men are good, yet whenever she's approached by a man who wants to date her she ignores his intentions, thinking that he must be as damaged as she. Furthermore, she believes, "if he really knew me he would think twice about asking me out for a date."

Fearful-Avoidants dodge emotional and sexual intimacy and disengage or distance themselves as a result of high anxiety and high avoidance in relationship. Their attempts to deflect or otherwise avoid deep feelings are most likely due to a violent and abusive childhood family system. However, Fearful-Avoidants cannot escape thinking about close relationships no matter how hard they try not to. Scientists refer to this as the "ironic rebound effect,"[3] similar to what would happen if someone said, "*Don't* think of a white horse."[4] Consequently, they tend to seek superficial physical/sexual encounters with others (e.g., anonymous sex, one-night stands, online sexual encounters, pornography, and the like).

Consider John from the initial example above. In early childhood John spent many nights alone, waiting for his single-parent mother to return from her second job as a janitor – which she took so she could support herself and her son. In this way John learned that in order to be loved and cared for he needed to endure loneliness. In other words, he learned that being loved also meant being abandoned. His upbringing is a perfect example of how terrifying childhood attachment figures can be, even when that terror is sometimes unintentional. Although his mother never intended any harm, her single mother status and the need for a second job conveyed this painful mixed message. As an adult John experiences so much internal distress and shame that he has become emotionally walled-off, preferring to remain alone rather than face the threat of "inevitable" abandonment.

DISMISSING-AVOIDANT ATTACHMENT STYLE (HIGH AVOIDANCE, LOW ANXIETY)

- Allison can barely contain herself when she tells her friends she's met a new guy online. She has always enjoyed her independence, so this long distance relationship is just what she wants. Besides, she says, "I don't like guys getting too attached. If they do I just move on to the next. I let them know this up front, so if they have a problem with that it won't matter."

- Jim is unsympathetic to his girlfriend's attempts to connect with him. She can't understand why he was so into her early on, and now he seems disinterested. In an effort to be emotionally intimate with Jim she has asked that he join her in counseling. His response is: "I'll go with you if that's what you really want, but I think it's a waste of our time and your money."

- "Relationships!" Brandon blurts out. "Do I really want to get involved with a relationship just to have great sex? I'm not that kind of guy. Give me gorgeous, self-sufficient women who don't need to be rescued, and I'm all in; that is until they want more. Then I'm out of there!"

Allison, Jim, and Michael are examples of dismissing-avoidant individuals. They are emotionally unavailable, and they actively disengage from real intimacy. People with a dismissing-avoidant adult attachment style often protect themselves with a wall of charm – a seductive manner that conveys interest but does not allow for deeper emotional and relational connection. If you've seen the movie *Shame*, the main character Brandon, (portrayed by Michael Fassbender) is a classic example of the charming yet dismissive-avoidant adult male. This sort of engaging behavior can be irresistibly alluring to the "neediness" of those with a preoccupied attachment style, as their need for attention and connection is fulfilled (temporarily) by the seductive yet walled off nature of the dismissive-avoidant.

In the last example above, Brandon's pursuit of gorgeous, self-sufficient women makes for an intense initial connection. The women he pursues perceive his strong, take-control attitude as alluring – perhaps even intoxicatingly so. Unfortunately, they also see it as a promise of a deeper emotional connection to come. What Brandon doesn't tell them is that after this initial early stage of hot sex he will not be invested in the connection or interested in developing the substantive emotional intimacy his female partner desires. His early focused attention on her delivers a promise of connection, but that promise will not be fulfilled.

In situations where Brandon sticks around past a one-night stand, he inevitably becomes uncomfortable with the closeness his partner seeks and the anxiety she displays when she doesn't get it. He may detach by engaging in substance addictions (drugs, food, and alcohol) or behavioral addictions (compulsive masturbation, anonymous sexual encounters, gambling, video gaming, shopping, work, and the like) in an attempt to create distance between him and his partner.

Needless to say, Brandon's inability to remain relational stems from childhood attachments that were either consistently unavailable or smothering. A child that experienced too little interaction learns to be self-sufficient and counter-dependent. It is important to note that emotional distance can also cause a person to become compulsively drawn or addicted to those people who are dismissive and avoidant as in, "I want what I cannot have!"

Although no childhood is perfect, "good enough" parenting makes the world of difference in how we learn and develop a healthy relationship with ourselves and others, as we read in the three examples of secure attachment. Conversely, of course, parenting that falls short of "good enough" can have a significant impact on later adult relationships. In this chapter we explored the experience of fear and anxiety in relationships.

In the following chapter we'll examine the powerful emotion of shame and its role in an attack on the self or another. Before you proceed consider the following questions:

~~~

QUESTIONS FOR YOURSELF:

- What is my own attachment style?

- How emotionally available were my caregivers in childhood?

- Do I seek distance or closeness in a relationship? How do I do that?

- Do I tolerate my own emotions?

- Do I numb my feelings? If so, how?

QUESTIONS ABOUT YOUR PARTNER:

- What is my partner's attachment style?

- How emotionally available were his or her caregivers in childhood?

- Does s/he tolerate their emotions?

- Does my partner seek closeness or create distance in a relationship? How?

- Does s/he numb their feelings? If so, how?

CHAPTER 2

SEX, SHAME, AND ANGER

Owning our story can be hard but not nearly as difficult as spending our lives running from it. Embracing our vulnerabilities is risky but not nearly as dangerous as giving up on love and belonging and joy—the experiences that make us the most vulnerable. Only when we are brave enough to explore the darkness will we discover the infinite power of our light.

— *Brené Brown*

Shannon is an executive with a large multinational corporation. She pierced the proverbial "glass ceiling" many years ago, at a time when women rarely held upper-level management positions. She became vice-president of development for a technology firm which is, even in today's progressive world, an anomaly in her male-dominated field. She is confident, self-assured, and rarely at a loss for words. These qualities continue to serve her well since her success has always been predicated on anticipating and foreseeing problems in her company's division.

Shannon's business associates and friends often hear her quip, "I get paid to predict the future, not prevent it."

She did not, however, foresee or even suspect the shocking news that her husband was having sex outside their marriage had it not been for her annual check-up with her gynecologist. During her annual visit the doctor spotted a small cyst around her genitalia. The doctor assured Shannon that it was probably nothing, but she nevertheless decided to run some tests. Two days after Shannon saw her doctor she received an unexpected phone call. "I'm really surprised but I have to tell you that your lab results came back positive for syphilis." Shannon was shocked – speechless, in fact. Her head was reeling. In addition to the shock of the news, she began to feel a creeping sense of humiliation; "how could I be so oblivious to what was going on with my own body," she thought! Yes, she knew that her husband Ted looked at pornography when she was away on business trips. In fact, she had confronted him on several occasions, letting him know she did not approve of the behavior. But she never once suspected that his porn use would or had led to in-the-flesh infidelity. Clearly, she thought, this must be the only possible explanation for her having an STD since she had never been unfaithful to Ted.

After receiving the phone call from her doctor, Shannon left the office to confront Ted at his place of work. Despite being presented with the news of Shannon's syphilis diagnosis, Ted maintained his innocence, going so far as to question Shannon's fidelity on her many business trips. It was only after seeing the extreme agony that Shannon was in that he acknowledged having gone, *on one occasion*, to an adult bookstore. Nevertheless, he maintained his innocence and showed only a measure of emotional support. Yes, he admitted, "I had gone to an adult bookstore but I have never been sexual with anyone!" He asserted his claim that he had only gone into the bookstore to "see what was there."

IF ONLY YOU KNEW ME!

Confronting sexual infidelity or compulsivity, be it your own or your partner's, is not for the faint of heart. Compulsive sexual acting out, especially when it reaches a level of sexual addiction, is a secretive, shame-filled world of pornography, prostitution, anonymous sexual encounters, voyeurism, exhibitionism, affairs, and a plethora of other "socially unacceptable" behaviors. Sharing or learning about the details of sexual betrayal can be awkward, frightening, scandalous, shaming, messy, muddled, rageful, chaotic, erotic, perverse, and more. And it is always complex, to say the least. Those who engage in such behaviors, as in Ted's case, are often too ashamed to disclose what they are doing, even when their activities are causing negative consequences in their lives or they are eventually confronted with the evidence. Similarly, partners of these individuals may opt to live in an "eyes wide shut" state, ignoring obvious signs and symptoms of their partner's ongoing sexual misbehavior.

On rare occasions sexually compulsive individuals do seek assistance on their own, and willingly disclose their many secrets in individual therapy or in group, as part of the recovery process. Typically, though, the decision is not so virtuous. A forced disclosure may become the result of an abrupt and un-ignorable discovery (such as an STD, in Shannon's case). This kind of a disclosure, however incomplete it might be, precipitates the immediate collapse of the addict's precariously perched house of cards. The resultant destruction of a secretive and shameful hidden life is highly traumatic for all concerned. For the addict, there is shock and fear that comes along with the slowly emerging exposure of his or her behavior. And for the partner, there is the trauma and shame about the newly discovered reality about the secret or level of secrets and betrayal.

For the sex addict, at the point of disclosure, these newly exposed secrets often become the "force majeure" that drives the addict to seek therapy, where s/he will hopefully confront their shame. Yet to be revealed is their loathing and self-disgust buried underneath the layers of sexually compulsive and newly exposed behaviors. Either way, the endless cover-ups, lies, deceit, and deceptions of this shame-filled netherworld cease to effectively work, as a spouse, partner, or some other person discovers the double life that the addict had up to now managed to adroitly shield from view.

At the same time of discovery the addict's partner's world also inextricably and traumatically changes as s/he becomes aware of at least some of the sordid details of the partner's addiction. In many cases the most traumatizing of all details is the fact that the addict's behavior may have likely played out, at least in part, right under the family's roof and for a longer period of time than s/he ever imagined.

Anger, pain, and shame following emotional and sexual betrayal is all but certain, and in the heat of the moment rage becomes the knee-jerk reaction for many traumatized partners in an all-out assault against the betrayal.

SHAME ON YOU!

Betrayed partners often resort to public disclosure of every sordid and scandalous detail in retaliation for their own hurt, pain, and shame. In the days that followed Shannon's shocking call from the doctor's office, she pieced together old emails, texts, and various undeleted online communications between Ted and his sex partners. It was clear to her right from the start that Ted was lying, but she wanted the irrefutable proof that she could use to confront him. What she found was that Ted, among other things, had been having sex with other men. This confused, and frightened her. Unfortunately, this and other discoveries pushed her into a searing abyss of pain, shame, and anger. Rather than confronting Ted, as she had initially planned, she composed an email, in which she attached many of his texts and online chats with his anonymous male sexual partners, and sent it as a massive email blast to all of his professional and personal contacts. In the moment, Shannon was determined to expose her husband as the scourge of the earth she now knew him to be. However, this impulsive decision became a bad idea that Shannon soon regretted.

Public displays of revenge and humiliation sometimes provide momentary gratification, but ultimately such retaliation is self-defeating and highly destructive. Shannon felt compelled to take action against her husband. What she was not prepared for was the professional and personal backlash against her for exposing him in such a public and scandalous manner. In the hours and days that followed, Shannon felt immeasurable shame and guilt about what she'd done, along with intensifying fury at her husband. All the while she experienced very little in the way of relief for her excruciating emotional pain or support from others about the events that led to her retaliation in the first place.

SHAME ON ME!

Surprising as this becomes, some betrayed partners direct shame and anger inward, blaming themselves for not having known that their spouse was acting out sexually. They find themselves thinking: "How could I not have known? I'm a bright and intelligent person, so how could this have happened without me suspecting?" Or, worse still, "How stupid am I for believing him (or her) – for *wanting* to believe him (or her)?" In such cases the betrayed partner takes on the shame of the addict's infidelity and deceit. "How could I be so – ?" (fill in self-deprecating adjective here.) This becomes the betrayed partner's traumatic mantra – repeated over and over until they come to grips with the reality that this self-directed shame is in reality the addict's to own and account for.

Sadly, for those who are mired in the trauma of sudden and unexpected discovery of a partner's sexual infidelity, it is tempting to own the shame and keep the betrayal a secret for fear of *what others might think*. Frequently the anger and shame surrounding such disclosure provokes internal anxiety reminiscent of past and unconscious memories of childhood. For many people, growing up in a dysfunctional and shaming environment means that to feel anger will cause potential rejection and abandonment by a caregiver. The betrayed partner fears that an overt display of anger will prompt immediate abandonment or, worse yet, rage followed by abandonment and rejection. This internal distress caused by such fears is typically fueled by past memories, both conscious and unconscious. In an attempt to restore internal calm, the betrayed partner wittingly or unwittingly turns the anger inward, feeding a downward spiral of shame, guilt, and internal rage. In *Shame & Guilt; Masters of Disguise*, Jane Middleton-Moz writes:

> *"We see adults submitting to the outrageous demands of partners or employers. We see individuals who appear to be constantly angry and then almost immediately, guilty. We see adults who have lifelong depression. The rage felt when shamed in childhood and when suffering from debilitating shame in adulthood, is turned against the self because of the dependency on the other for survival. When we are rejected in adulthood by a mate or a lover, the feelings we experience are anger at being rejected. Furthermore, if we suffer from debilitating shame, we have not been able to gain autonomy."*

In other words, a newly discovered sexual infidelity can for some become the externalized proof of what a betrayed partner may have secretly believed about himself or herself since early childhood – *I am not good enough. I am not worthy. I am unlovable*. Only now the curtain has been pulled back exposing this horrible truth for the entire world to see.

Consider the case of Carla, who called me after learning of her husband's serial extramarital affairs. Carla's 15-year marriage was not perfect by any means. She and her husband Dan had struggled with maintaining intimacy since their children were born. That said, now that their children were 12, 8, and 6, Carla had begun to feel "herself" again. She was committed to exercising and eating right and her body was returning to its pre-pregnancy shape. In short, she was feeling good about herself. But her burgeoning self-worth dissolved when she stumbled upon her husband's phone replete with emails and website profiles for sexual encounters. She couldn't believe that her husband could have cheated on her, but there was the evidence in all its glory – emails, hookup apps, porn websites, dating websites, even a profile on Ashley Madison (a website and app designed specifically for extramarital hookups). Dan's recent compliments about how good she looked lately now seemed like hollow adulation. It was clear that Dan was actively engaged in a series of sexual affairs. Sadly, as is all too often the case with partners, Carla felt guilty about discovering Dan's secret, as if his betrayal and deceit was somehow hers to atone for.

Rather than feeling anger at Dan for his betrayal, Carla felt shame toward herself. She tried hard to get angry, but could only feel guilt and remorse for spying on Dan by looking at his phone. And adding to this trauma were Carla's many proclamations to friends and family that her marriage, unlike others, was strong, healthy, and emotionally close. How many times had she told her girlfriends, "Dan couldn't be sweeter or more loving. I'm so lucky!"

On her initial visit to me Carla openly regretted her self-perceived stupidity. Carla was consumed by a shame spiral, lamenting, "My girl-friends at the club will never understand this, especially since I've been bragging about how Dan is such a wonderful husband and father. We've even been planning to renew our vows! I feel so stupid. I'm a laughing stock."

So rather than lashing out at her cheating husband as Shannon did with hers, Carla turned her anger inward, struggling to see that Dan's behavior was *his* to own. For Carla, hiding the truth about her marriage (and, in the process, blaming herself for her husband's choices) was preferable to disclosure of this potentially humiliating and shameful secret. The fact that she had been unaware of what was happening only compounded her shame and self-loathing. Also troubling to me, as a therapist, was Carla's core belief that her body, her weight, and her self-perceived unattractiveness must have been the cause for Dan's sexual acting out. *If I was good enough Dan would not have strayed.*

ONE UP / ONE DOWN

Holding the addict's shame in lieu of holding the addict accountable is, unfortunately, what happens with many betrayed partners. I have found over the years that spouses who grew up in shame-based and rigid family systems share a predisposition toward holding the shame and relegating themselves to the *Shameful* and *One Down* position in the relationship. This compensatory act both consciously and unconsciously manifests an internal sense of unworthiness that predates the marriage and stems from childhood. As seen in Figure 2. below, the source of the shame is the same for the betrayer as it is for the betrayed – a shame core.

However, for the betrayed partner relegating oneself to *Shameful* and *One Down* is an old and natural default and, therefore, preferable. This one down position is a more life- preserving stance since it does not require confrontation. In essence, to confront the betrayer would force the betrayed partner to also confront his or her own sense of shame, anger, pain, fear, and self-doubt about ever being "good enough." From this one-down position a betrayed partner has learned to comfortably dwell in the "land of the shameful."

Although the cheating partner's *Shameless* and *One Up* position stems from and is driven by the same shame core, the addict manifests his or her low self-worth with a counteractive stance of "better than." This self-entitled narcissistic facade is a compensatory albeit thinly veiled offensive measure against his or her fragile self-esteem and being "not good enough." Adopting the default position of *Shameless* and *One Up* ultimately bolsters rather than diminishes his or her internal feeling of less than, despite the outwardly projected mastery of self. The cheating partner's shameless behavior becomes the maladaptive equalizing counterpoint to the betrayed partner's shameful one-down position in the relationship. But the newly exposed secrets of a "perfect" life are now flayed open.

Figure 2. Adapted from Pia Mellody's Post
Induction Training

The shamelessness of the compulsive and potentially denied behavior is held by the betrayed partner and taken on as his or her identity—the cheater's covert shame becomes the betrayed partner's overt shame—his or her "cross to bear." Sometimes the betrayer feeds into this, proclaiming, "How could you not have known?" How could you have believed me? Didn't you realize that what I was telling you couldn't possibly have made sense?" This type of sadistic and narcissistic attack all but compels a betrayed partner into self-doubt and blame. Unfortunately, in such cases the betrayed partner is no more capable now than he or she was before of filtering sincerity from insincerity, reality from fabrication. The partner reels, the family is thrown into turmoil, and all involved face the unwelcome task of picking up the pieces.

WHEN THERE IS NO NORMAL

As mentioned earlier, sex addicts and others who engage in compulsive sexual behaviors may seek help on their own, without some dire consequence or discovery driving them into treatment. This, however, is extremely rare. The more common scenario is the addict phones for help in an effort to save something near and dear to him: his marriage, job, or reputation. Kurt is one such individual. One afternoon he called me and said, "I'd like to come in and meet with you. We've had some problems in our marriage and I'm living with a friend because my wife discovered pornography and a stash of saved emails on my laptop. You know the usual stuff."

I quickly asserted there is no such thing as usual stuff.

"Well, yeah, anyway, she threw me out of the house. I need to make an appointment as soon as possible. I want to put my family back together. I might have already lost them, but hopefully not. I need to try and figure out what's going on." His voice started to shake when he said, "I'm not sure that it's possible to save my marriage, but I'll do anything, anything to try!"

I wasn't sure if Kurt was upset at what he had done, or upset that he had gotten caught and was now facing serious consequences. My first thought about calls such as Kurt's is, "they may be in crisis but they may not be in pain." Kurt wanted to come to therapy to alleviate the crisis but did he want to work beyond that to tackle the real problem? Frankly, it didn't matter. Just making the call, whatever the reason, was an act of courage and, on some level, an admission of shame. For a sex addict – and I later came to diagnose Kurt as such – walking into a therapist's office and disclosing closely guarded secrets about one's highly shameful fantasies and behaviors is a powerful leap of faith. Of course, for that step to be taken the addict must feel comfortable in his or her therapist's presence. Existentialist psychotherapist and author Irvin D. Yalom once wrote:

> *"The closeness of the therapy relationship serves*
> *many purposes. It affords a safe place for the patients to*
> *reveal themselves as fully as possible. More than that, it*
> *offers them the experience of being accepted and under-*
> *stood after deep disclosure. It teaches social skills: The*
> *patient learns what an intimate relationship requires.*
> *And the patient learns that intimacy is possible, even*
> *achievable."*[1]

This means that as a therapist I must be able to sit comfortably with my client's shame. Of course, in order to do that I needed to first learn what it was like to sit with my own. And prior to recovery, I could not do that. In fact, I didn't even know what shame really was or that I had any, let alone that my shame was manifesting in my daily life. I was simply unaware of how shame looked, felt, and manifested, and that it was profoundly affecting my life. At any given time I was prepared to counter my internal running belief – *I am a mistake* – in whatever way was necessary, whether it was healthy or not. And on the rare occasions where that belief came to light I became a raging behemoth, fighting like a wild-woman to beat back that belief, away from the light of day.

OUT OF SIGHT; OUT OF MIND

Today when I sit in empathic witness to my clients' struggles, allowing individuals like Kurt to unravel and experience the shame of their acting out, often for the first time, I know that I am able to do so only because I have experienced my own shame, venturing deeper than I ever dreamed possible to confront what was safely hidden from view. At first stoically, then courageously, I learned how to lean into the intensity of my own humiliation, which had forever breathed life into the words "stupid and ugly." That internal message of defectiveness was once upon a time enough to toss me into a shame spiral of great magnitude.

I remember the early days in my personal work when walking into a self-help (twelve-step) meeting conjured more fear than walking in my own addict's shadow. I remember feeling that the only safe haven in the world existed in the corner of my therapist's office. Ignore me. I'll just curl up in a fetal position and be real quiet – I won't say a word. Just pretend I'm not even here. Really – I just need to be here and soak up the safety. Over time I learned that the only way out of that struggle was through it, so I walked one day at a time, sometimes even one hour at a time, into the distant light, eventually emerging as a happier, healthier human being. That small beacon of hope grew into the serenity in which I live today.

But, over time and through much effort, I found a place of compassion for myself that ultimately turned into healthy pride and self-love. It is my hope that each individual remains in therapy long enough to learn that their shame most likely stems from their unresolved childhood trauma or neglect, and that shame is what feeds his or her raging inner scorn.

In my practice I find that most of my clients, especially the sex addicts, are, as I was, unaware that they even hold shame, let alone that it is rooted in their past and affecting their present. The level of knowing that ongoing recovery provides only comes with time and certainly not until the person has entered into withdrawal and abstinence from addictive behaviors This is because the cauterizing effects of addictions all but deaden the emotions of pain, shame, guilt, loneliness, and anger, keeping addicts deeply disconnected from any conscious contact with reality.

Therapists who work with addiction – sex addiction in particular – know what lies buried beneath the surface, the secrets that fuel the odious shame and feed the raging sexual compulsivity. We are also aware that those active in their sex addiction will keep coming up against themselves and their process until they finally decide to stop what they are doing and confront their hidden, dark side. But how their process came to be and how they act out or re-enact their sexual proclivities reflects an older, oftentimes disowned past. On a daily basis, one by one, in quiet, oftentimes reluctant and begrudging fashion, men and women come to me for therapeutic guidance and healing. In so doing, they are taking a courageous leap of faith into the abyss of their unknown.

Shannon, Carla, and Kurt began their path of self-examination without much warning or time for planning. The events that hurled them into a new and harrowing chapter of their lives were borne out of different circumstances and life decisions that were no less important for each of them to make. Shannon and Carla had decisions to make about themselves, their marriages, and their core values. Kurt needed to decide if he truly wanted to change or just engage in damage control.

Regardless of our circumstances, if we fail to surrender to self-exploration and internal examination we remain enslaved to the corrosive effects of buried shame, be it our own or another's. Finding the courage to look inward and make changes speaks to what we value both for ourselves and in our relationships. In the next chapter we will take a look at what that means. However, consider the role that shame may play in your professional and personal relationships.

~~~

QUESTIONS FOR YOURSELF:

- Do I love myself?

- Do I like myself?

- How do I express shame?

- In relationships do I occupy the Shameless/one-up or Shameful/one-down position?

- In *our* relationship what position do I occupy?

QUESTIONS ABOUT YOUR PARTNER:

- Does my partner like him/herself?

- Does s/he love himself or herself?

- How does s/he express shame?

- In a personal or professional relationship does my partner occupy the Shameless/one-up or Shameful/one-down position?

- In *our* relationship what shame position does my partner occupy?

CHAPTER 3
YOUR RELATIONAL CURRENCY

Money, it turned out, was exactly like sex, you thought of nothing else if you didn't have it and thought of other things if you did.

—James A. Baldwin

Some years back when I was deep into my own therapy, I explored why I stayed in a marriage that was no longer satisfying, no longer loving, and painful. My husband and I had fallen not just out of love, but out of appreciation. Perhaps the value of appreciation and the commitment to expressing it was never there, with that lack masked by other more emergent desires such as growing our careers, making our mark in the business world and living a comfortable life. What we truly valued and how we expressed that was only exposed by the glaring void created when we were no longer vested in seeing eye-to-eye. At that point, the fact that we'd grown out of appreciation became all too obvious. We had strayed from the love and appreciation that drew us together initially, and in therapy I was intent on exploring the how and the why of that. I wasn't interested in the blame game; I was interested in *why I chose to stay* despite what was no longer there.

When two people come together under an emotional and erotic cosmic trance, the one question they most likely don't ask is: "What do I value most about being in a relationship?" This makes sense, given that our brains are hijacked by the hormonal and chemical rush of lust and attraction. Hopefully those conversations do occur, but later, after the lustful phase known as limerence subsides and the rose-colored glasses come off. This is where the relational currency begins to develop.

SEX APPEAL AS CURRENCY

Currency is generally thought of as a form of economic or monetary exchange (i.e., money). But currency needn't be pieces of paper or coins accepted as legal national tender. Currency can also be the emotional and sexual cache a person brings to a relationship. This type of relational currency speaks to what we value, our relational strengths, and the ways in which we communicate our values and strengths to a loved one. In other words, relational currency is the acts and statements used to express love and affection in relationship.

In the early phase of connection, when we are star-crossed lovers, we don't barter in deeper relational currency, the proverbial life questions about what we truly value, or at least we are not likely to do so. These questions tend to surface about our romantic partner much later, often under a cloud of exasperation or relational disconnect. How is my partner showing up in our relationship, how does my partner express love and affection, and what does my partner value in the relationship?

We also ask these same questions of ourselves, albeit less often. In what ways am *I* showing up in our relationship, how do *I* express love and affection toward my partner and what do I value in the relationship? I often hear these and other statements in my work with couples:

- He may not be very handsome, but the truth is that I married him for his money and he married me for my looks.

- If he would only tell me that he even cares about me or loves me I wouldn't feel so alone. But at least I get to live a rich lifestyle.

- My friends are so envious that I'm engaged to a successful and handsome man. They tell me that it's normal to be afraid about marriage and that I have nothing to complain about. But they don't know that he is insecure and when things get rough, he drinks and takes off to the bars with his friends.

- My wife stopped having sex with me years ago. So should I have stopped paying the bills?

- Sure I know that he drinks, looks at porn and goes to strip clubs. Don't all men do that? Besides, I love to spend money and I'm not prepared to give that up.

In 2010, Dr. Catherine Hakim, a British sociologist, presented a theory on what she called "erotic capital." Hakim wrote, "Erotic capital combines beauty, sex appeal, liveliness, a talent for dressing well, charm and social skills, and sexual competence. Rather than degrading those who employ it, erotic capital represents a powerful and potentially equalizing tool – one that we scorn only to our own detriment." [1] In other words, the use of sex, sex appeal, and beauty as currency in courtships and relationships has long been a part of mating and dating. Prostitution, for instance, dates back to at least 2400 B.C. [2] Controversial or not, Hakim's perspective clearly identifies a longstanding tool of relational influence. Putting the matter as simply as possible sex appeal has always been, either overtly or covertly, used as relational currency, and this is likely to continue ad infinitum.

'TIL THEFT DO US PART

Money is also used, rather routinely, as currency in relationships. This is an all too common theme in sessions with couples. One particular session comes to mind.

"I make the money and you spend it." Chuck said to his wife Katie. He was self-righteously angry, and all too happy to express his anger to a sympathetic ear and audience – me.

"I don't remember vowing 'til theft do us part,'" he added. "I don't remember that we actually decided this. So maybe this was one of your unilateral marital decisions you made while I wasn't looking."

"Sorry you weren't there, Chuck." Katie retorted. "You must have been 'burning the midnight oil'. Or is that burning the midnight oil with your colleague?"

That brought the discussion to a screeching halt, and we sat in silence. I tried not to smile at the dark humor Katie sometimes wielded when she was particularly hurt.

Given that Katie had asked for a crisis session and they were here to discuss Chuck's latest infidelity, I was a bit surprised that they'd veered off on this money-related tangent. And yet I wasn't surprised at all.

Chuck and Katie had married 14 years ago in better times. The economy hadn't yet eroded their life savings, their house had not come under the threat of foreclosure, and Chuck's smoldering predilection for escorts and inter-office affairs hadn't yet surfaced. Now money was tight, and both were spending it recklessly – Chuck on illicit sex, Katie on clothes and home furnishings. Both partners had been wielding the couple's strained finances as a weapon for quite some time, so it was inevitable that we'd finally get around to this topic.

As is common for many in relationships, one of the partners comes to therapy in hopes of resolving an issue that has become problematic, perhaps even hopeless – in this case Chuck's infidelity. Chuck was aware that Katie was unhappy and that she wanted to come to therapy to discuss his cheating. But in moments such as this, the therapist's office becomes a *de facto* safe zone for what I call the relational rummage sale, meaning that eventually everything in the relationship ends up displayed – or as it was – flayed on the table. Once "safely" inside the therapy room, a partner or spouse drags out all the *stuff* that's been stored for years in his or her emotional attic. Out comes the debris: long-standing resentments, fetid secrets, dashed hopes and disappointments that were, in their day, prized treasures and celebratory relational jewels.

For Chuck and Katie, this couldn't have been truer. Katie had called and scheduled the appointment to "deal with Chuck's latest sexual betrayal," but when the door opened and the opportunity to expose unsung grievances presented it was game on. Resentments that had been festering for years were suddenly out in the open, ready to be picked over, looked at, discussed, and hopefully, in time, discarded.

Several minutes passed while Chuck and Katie sat in silence, avoiding even a glance at the other. Finally, Katie glanced anxiously at me, looking for some sort of sign that would communicate to her, "Go ahead, you have my permission to continue." My silence was intentional. I was curious as to where this session was really heading. Suddenly Katie forged ahead.

"What do you mean 'til theft do us part? If you mean that I spend the money, I do. That's my job, isn't it? I'm the one at home with the kids. I get them set for school and take care of the doctors' visits, clothes, you know EVERYTHING. And *everything* is also what I gave up in order to stay home and raise the kids. Well, I'm tired of that. I'm tired of doing everything! I buy the food, keep the house, manage everything, and all you do is go to work and apparently screw around with any woman that will have you, and then you come home and sit on your ass like you've fulfilled all your daily requirements!"

Katie turned toward me and told me that Chuck had no idea about half of what went on at home, as if Chuck himself was not inches from her and within earshot of that very gibe. At this point I finally interjected. "I'm confused. I thought we're here today because of Chuck's infidelity. Is that the case? Or are there more pressing issues?"

MONEY MATTERS

According to a national telephone survey conducted in early 2012 by Harris Interactive for the American Institute of Certified Public Accountants (AICPA), financial matters are the most common cause of discord among American couples.[3] Twenty-seven percent of those who are married or living with a partner acknowledged that disagreements over money are the most likely cause of a spat, causing an average of three arguments per month. Financial matters topped the list, beating out children, chores, sex, work, friends, and every other potential bone of contention. "According to the survey, much of a relationship's financial conflict can be traced to a failure to communicate about money matters. Amazingly, 55 percent of the people surveyed admitted that they do not set aside time on a regular basis to talk about financial issues."

About the study's findings, Jordan Amin, chair of the National CPA Financial Literacy Commission, said, "Money is a lightning rod for conflict in relationships because it's a sensitive topic and each person brings a different perspective based on their past experiences. It's critical for couples to communicate openly and regularly about financial matters in order to establish a common language around money and move toward shared goals." Unfortunately, most couples, like Chuck and Katie in the discussion above, do not heed Amin's advice. And when they don't, financial matters can create silent resentments that manifest badly in any number of ways.

It seems logical that if financial matters are the primary source of discord among couples, then relational currency should be the primary avenue for exploring how couples relate. In my practice I have found this to absolutely be the case. The simple fact is that couples arrive at a relational medium of exchange, whether they know it or not. This relational currency is based on their individual values (both conscious and unconscious).

In therapy sessions, the fact that everyone has values is not in dispute. What is up for discussion is what those values are, and whether they've become the proverbial tail wagging the relational dog.

Discovering what each partner values – really values, and is ultimately seeking in marriage or relationship and then negotiating for it – is paramount to relational success or failure. I have often shared with clients that in relationships there are two types of information: the information we need to know and have yet to ask for, and the information we already have yet choose to ignore. Actively discovering, accepting, and dealing with a person's relational currency is difficult to do in the limerence of early sexual and emotional discovery. Most of us enjoy basking in the excitement and exhilaration of a promising relationship. When we ignore obvious information or continue to avoid asking important life questions, this promising relationship is threatened from the outset.

WHAT ARE WE REALLY FIGHTING FOR?

During their therapy session, Chuck and Katie sparred about sexual infidelity and money. However, as the therapeutic process unfolded over the next few months, other underlying needs and values (relational currency) came to light. As it turns out, twenty years earlier, when Chuck and Katie were dating, Chuck was quick to point out much of what he so adored about Katie: her quick wit, her ability to hold her own in negotiations with her male business colleagues, and her needless/wantless stance. What he kept secret at that time, only revealing it in a therapy session, was that he'd also been attracted to Katie's youth, as she was 10 years his junior. Reading between the lines it was easy to deduce that part of Chuck's relational currency was: I'll provide the salary if you keep providing the looks.

Katie's relational currency was slightly different. Early on she was enamored with Chuck's lithe social ease and his ability to make conversation in any situation, be it in business or in a social realm. Katie valued this part of Chuck's life because it extended social standing. It was also Chuck's established financial success that Katie found so appealing. As time passed, however, Katie seemed to forget that Chuck's success in business is part of what made him so attractive to her in the first place. When the financial crash began in 2008, their finances were greatly impacted and it was clear to me that this major financial upheaval had as much to do with her anger at Chuck as his serial infidelity.

It seems that Katie and Chuck's values, their relational currency, became over time deficits and aspects of mutual disdain. I knew that if they were to ever find their way back to their early relational roots, both would have to work at being honest with themselves, honest with the other, and sharing equally in the heavy lifting of therapy. Regardless of the internal work to be done, external distractions and Chuck's readily apparent (to me) sexual addiction would need to be dealt with immediately.

Interestingly, Chuck and Katie were in much the same situation as I was when I first entered recovery. For years I had been blissfully, and then not-so-blissfully unaware of what I truly valued in a relationship. It took time and hard work in therapy before I realized that I had never asked the important life questions of myself (let alone of my husband), primarily because I had no idea what those questions were. I was not self-aware. And, unfortunately, had I known the questions and asked them he would not have been able to answer, as he was not in an emotional place to see life honestly. My hard-won self-insight may have come too late to save my marriage, but, happily, it arrived just in time for the rest of my life.

Below is a short list of life questions I pose to couples as they begin their individual and couples work in therapy. As you answer these questions refer to Chapter One for attachment styles. Being acquainted with yours and your partner's patterns of attachment will help you better understand the patterns of connection and avoidance.

~~~

QUESTIONS FOR YOURSELF:

- What do I value in a relationship?

- Do I ask for what I need and want?

- How do I express love and affection in my relationships?

- How do I show my love and affection to my partner?

- Do I express my love for him/her in a way that s/he values?

QUESTIONS ABOUT YOUR PARTNER:

- What does my partner really value in a relationship?

- Is my partner emotionally available in the ways that I need and want?

- Does my partner express love and affection in the ways that I need/want?

- How does s/he show his/her love and affection for me?

- Does my partner express his/her love for me in ways that I value?

CHAPTER 4
EMOTIONAL SCARCITY - SEXUAL SURPLUS

Regulars use fantasy to cover over the material reality of their interactions with dancers...Success for dancers requires that they must appear to the customer as their fantasy object in an unproblematic way.

– R. Danielle Egan,
Dancing for Dollars and Paying for Love

Sex addiction is not about the sex. To describe sex addiction as simply compulsive sexual behavior profoundly underestimates addiction in general, not to mention the specific nuances of sexual fantasy and behavior. The same can be said for addictive spending, alcoholism, drug abuse, compulsive gambling, eating disorders, and the like. The substance or process to which one is addicted speaks to the individual's perceived *need for escape* from *underlying and unresolved psychological* *issues.* In other words, addiction (in all its many forms) is a coping mechanism used to escape and dissociate from uncomfortable emotions and situations, along with issues like depression and severe anxiety. Addictive behaviors may start out as fun diversions, but they eventually become little more than a way to numb out. Left untreated, the progression of the abuse turns to dependence and then addiction. As I've heard many of my clients say, addicts don't engage in their addiction to feel better, they do it to feel less.

When we speak about addiction in general and sex addiction in particular, and you've gotten this far, then you already know that seduction is not connection and intensity is not intimacy – although at times intimacy can be intense. Chapter One, "Sex, Love, and Attachment," explored how unresolved trauma and patterns of childhood attachment influence our adult relationships. To extend that discussion a bit, children who don't learn to attach securely in infancy and childhood often carry into adulthood this inability to emotionally or spiritually connect with another human being. Sometimes for these individuals the experience of escape – either toward intensity or away from it – will prevail and become their primary coping mechanism. Instead of getting their needs met in healthy ways with the help of significant others (spouses, partners, and the like), these people turn to sexual fantasy (porn, strippers, and the like) and behaviors (affairs, compulsive masturbation, prostitutes) to mask any emotional needs.

When left untreated, this type of compulsive sexual acting out often goes awry. One needs only to perform an Internet search using the words *sex* and *scandal* to confirm this. In 2010, for example, the Business Insider website displayed the headline, "Deutsche Banker's Kinky Torture Fantasy Ends In Death."[1] Apparently, the assistant vice-president of a major bank had recently been laid off. As it turns out, for quite some time he had been soliciting escorts to help him fulfill his sexual torture fantasy. Reports into his death revealed that he had previously hired escorts to fulfill the following sexual fantasy:

"I want them to pretend they are executioners who are going to kill me. I want them to abuse me by saying I am a useless waste of space who deserves to die. I'll have a noose around my neck. Then they kick the stool from under my feet, laugh, and walk away without looking back."[1]

Whether his sexual fantasy resulted in an intentional suicide or sexual role play gone seriously wrong may never be determined. What is, however, of note is the banker's desire for sexual arousal resulting from shame and humiliation. His last reported text on the request to the escort service read: *"My crime is being a loser."*[2]

In retrospect the banker's shame core developed early and advanced throughout his life. Sadder still was that he carried it with him and sexually reenacted this childhood wound throughout his life, all the way to its tragic end. One wonders if he ever realized what he was feeling or doing, or if he ever sought therapy? If he did seek therapy, were his attachment issues and shame ever properly addressed?

Closer to current day and at the time of this writing, former New York state representative, turned New York City mayoral candidate, Anthony Weiner, has admitted, yet again, to sending sexually explicit messages online. This new development and public disclosure comes two years after an initial discovery called for his then congressional resignation. In a recent article published in The Washington Post, Anthony Weiner was cited as saying, "I am continuing to get professional help for my behavior but I do not consider my online dalliances to be an addiction."[3]

It's a sticky wicket when a client presents with compulsive sexual issues that are almost certainly related to unconscious, unresolved trauma. The emphasis at this point becomes addressing the out-of-control sexual acting while simultaneously considering the underlying trauma that is most likely fueling the sexual behavior.

I know from personal experience that it can be very difficult to maintain the delicate balance of hope counterpointed by the harsh reality of the work at hand, which involves a great deal of shameful disclosure and emotional pain. For anyone, a journey from sexual addiction into recovery takes time, effort, and considerable perseverance.

I could not sit where I do in the therapist's chair had I not first spent time on a therapist's couch. I learned first-hand how I used people, places and things to escape the intolerable. The only way I can help my clients (and therefore, they can help themselves) will be to help them lean into their discomfort in lieu of running from it. This involves giving up the maladaptive forms of escape that they have employed for their entire lives, In return they will learn how to lean into discomfort and use healthy coping mechanisms.

A lot of times my clients are still active in their addiction when they arrive in treatment. In such cases we work together to help them abstain from their addictive behaviors long enough to feel – emotions, life, and most of what they have avoided. Without this first-order component of sobriety, little progress can be made elsewhere.

> *The initial journey towards sobriety is a delicate balance between insight into one's desire for escape and abstinence from one's addiction.*

JACK

Jack, a construction manager, came to see me after he had been in recovery for five years for his sex addiction. "I'm in recovery for online porn, compulsive masturbation and fantasy, but I'm backsliding into my old ways," he told me. He acknowledged that after remaining abstinent from his bottom line sexual behaviors (activities that mean an addict has lost his or her sexual sobriety) he had begun to call upon his internally stored fantasies of past sexual conquests in order to escape life on life terms and to feel better about himself.

FRANK

Frank, a prominent CEO, was completely new to the notion of therapy when he came to see me in a crisis. In Frank's case, he was in crisis but he was not in pain. In our first session, despite his recent near-arrest for public indecency, Frank stated flatly that he had no intention of stopping his frequent bisexual encounters or his equally frequent anonymous public sex, which he said he engaged in as a way to relieve the stress of his high-pressure career. Soon thereafter, the fear caused by his near-arrest dissipated and he'd returned to thinking that he didn't really have a problem. Thus, there was nothing for us to officially work on. And if there *was* something to deal with, Frank seemed to think that merely showing up for therapy (apparently conducted and completed in one session) would solve the problem, whatever that problem might be. Though it may have seemed rather pointless, we were both there, so we gave it the old college try.

I learned that Frank was a hard-driving and ambitious man who rarely exposed his vulnerability. It was only in that brief moment of crisis prompted by the near-arrest that he called for an appointment. Without prompting, he referred to his behaviors as *deep* and *dark*. From that and similar statements it was obvious to me that his sexually compulsive behaviors were perpetuating a cycle of shame and secrecy that isolated him from colleagues, friends, and loved ones. And all the while he remained unaware as to what was driving his compulsions. Frank disclosed that while losing his family would be difficult it was less of a threat than losing his career. "The loss to his career," he stated, "would be a loss equal to none."

Despite his prolific and reckless sexual behavior, neither his wife nor his business partners knew of his activities. Furthermore, he was certain that he could successfully maintain this compartmentalization of his life. This belief alone was for him reason enough to continue his sexual acting out.

This sort of defiant invulnerability is common among sex addicts; they simply don't think they're ever going to get caught. Yes, a near-arrest will scare them and perhaps prompt them to briefly attempt change, but often it takes something far more catastrophic to induce lasting effort. Part of this invulnerability stems from the fact that admitting vulnerability is something most sex addicts avoid at all costs; otherwise they would try to develop and maintain true intimacy in their romantic relationships. In Frank's case admitting vulnerability would mean facing his worst fear and most destructive core beliefs: *I am weak and I'm a failure.*

ELLEN

Ellen was new to therapy but not to twelve-step recovery when she came to see me. "My sponsor in AA told me that I should look at my behaviors with men and relationships. I guess I like to flirt with men and seduce them, but I don't think it's a problem. It's such a rush! I don't necessarily intend to carry through with anything. I just like that feeling of power and control when I know that I've gotten their attention. Any time I'm feeling bad about myself, flirting with a guy and making him want me lifts my spirits."

EMOTIONAL SCARCITY

Sexual activity, with its inherent demand for physical and psychological intimacy, often creates discomfort for avoidant people, who, by their very nature, habitually seek physical and emotional distance from their partners. Their attempts to avoid intimacy typically manifest in one of two ways: either they abstain from any sexual activity (involving other people), or they engage in emotion-free sex via disengaged, short-term relationships (prostitutes, anonymous sex, one-night stands, and the like).

Research conducted at the Interdisciplinary Center Herzliya, School of Psychology in Israel explored the complex interplay between attachment processes and the sexual aspects of romantic love. According to psychologist and lead researcher, Gurit E. Birnbaum, "more avoidant individuals, in contrast, feel uncomfortable with the closeness inherently involved in sexual interactions and, therefore, tend to detach sexuality from psychological intimacy. This detached stance may account for diverse avoidance related sexual behaviors and motives, such as experiencing sexual fantasies in which they and the object of their fantasies are represented as interpersonally distant and alienated engaging in less-frequent sexual activities with relationship partners, reliance on the solitary sexual activity of masturbation, engaging in emotion-free sex (e.g., one-night stands; sex with casual partners), and having sex for relationship-irrelevant, self-enhancing reasons. When more avoidant people do have sex with their romantic partners, they tend to experience relatively strong feelings of estrangement and alienation and display low levels of physical affection. Overall, more avoidant individuals seem to have a sex life relatively devoid of affectional bonding, even within the context of ongoing romantic relationships."[4]

Additional research conducted by Dr. Birnbaum involved both members of 48 couples. In this study both individuals were asked to independently report their daily sex fantasies and relationship interactions with their partners for 21 days. The researchers were hoping to determine if each partner seemed to desire more closeness (attachment anxiety) or distance (avoidant attachment) in their relationship. Patterns suggested that the content of each sexual fantasy was directly influenced by the partner's personality, the quality of the relationship, and whether the couples' interaction for that day was positive or negative. Psychologist and lead researcher Gurit E. Birnbaum said, "On days when couples argued, both partners were more likely to have sexual fantasies about people other than their partner."[5]

Of particular note in the study was that avoidant men tended to fantasize about being sexually satisfied and irresistibly desired by unknown women. According to Birnbaum and her team, "this kind of fantasy may be a distancing strategy that minimizes intimacy and reflects a desire to escape."[6]

BIRDS OF THE SAME FEATHER

What Jack, Frank and Ellen all share is sexual addiction and emotional scarcity. Their search for intensity instead of intimacy keeps them trapped in a never-ending cycle of loneliness. Unique to each of them, however, was an individual love map – the map or path by which they consciously or unconsciously played out their unresolved past trauma, sexualized anger, shame, and anxiety. The concept of a love map was originated by John Money, a psychologist, sexologist and author. He specialized in research about sexual identity and biology of gender and used the term to help explain why people like what they enjoy sexually and erotically.[7] Patrick Carnes, Ph.D., a leading researcher and author in the field of sexual addiction, describes an arousal template similar to a love map in this way:

> *"The Arousal Template is a constellation, map or story comprised of thoughts, images, sights, sounds and fantasies – all stimuli that one finds arousing. The stored stimuli become fused with sexual arousal and consequently become the blueprint or template by which historical repetition and sexual arousal merge to become sexually reenacted."* [8]

Deconstructing one's arousal template is the fastest and most effective way to understand what drives compulsive sexual behaviors and, by extension, the ways in which undisclosed trauma, shame, and desire manifest in the here and now. As I described earlier, those with a fearful-avoidant attachment style are likely to seek out low contact sexual interaction such as online chats, webcam sex, or exhibitionistic/voyeuristic behaviors. In Chapter One, "Sex, Love, and Attachment," we learned about attachment styles and the ways in which an individual seeks either distance or proximity in relational behaviors. While it is necessary to consider one's attachment style when exploring sexual arousal, it is helpful to first examine the types of sexual arousal through the lens of the ten types of sexual arousal first identified by Dr. Carnes.

In the original research conducted by Dr. Carnes and researchers for his 1991 book, *Don't Call It Love*, a total of 10 "types" of sexually addictive behavior emerged in the sex addicts surveyed. "Those types included: Anonymous Sex, Exhibitionist Sex, Exploitive Sex, Fantasy Sex, Intrusive Sex, Pain Exchange Sex, Paying for Sex, Seductive Role Sex, Trading Sex, and Voyeuristic Sex." [9]

DECONSTRUCTING AROUSAL

Deconstructing a person's arousal template is both interesting and useful to the person's long-term recovery. Consider Ellen. In her individual and group work Ellen began to deconstruct her patterns of behavior through the lens of stored stimuli, emotions, and sexual proclivities. What was of particular interest was how her early patterns of attachment and unresolved trauma coalesced into patterns of reenacted conscious and unconscious sexual behavior. See Figure 3:

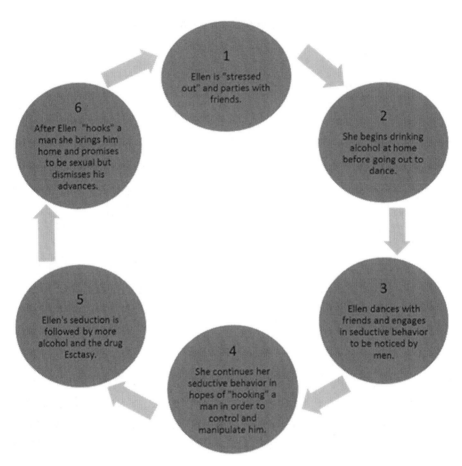

Figure 3. Adapted from Patrick Carnes, Ph.D., Arousal
Template.

In Ellen's childhood she experienced significant abandonment. Her father left the family when she was seven years old and she subsequently endured physical and sexual abuse by her step-father which lasted, off and on, for five years. Every bit as wounding as the actual abuse and abandonment was the fact that Ellen's mother did not protect her from her step-father. It took years before Ellen had the courage to tell someone who actually intervened on her behalf.

As Ellen grew older she began to drink to quell her intensifying pain and shame. In times of stress she often resorted to carving into her arm with a small paring knife followed by soothing compulsive masturbation. In her adult years, before she worked at being sober from drugs and alcohol, she began to act out her inner turmoil by seducing and then dismissing men. She disinhibited her pain and shame with alcohol and drugs and thereby became more free to express her sexualized rage by controlling and manipulating men. It was during these episodes that Ellen would outwardly perpetrate the rage and shame that she had been inwardly inflicting on herself. When she became sober from drugs and alcohol, Ellen's unresolved trauma was able to surface, no longer blocked or numbed by years of self-medicating.

Our work on her arousal template allowed for Ellen to clearly see her motives and intentions. This difficult work allowed her to recognize how she sexualized her anger and shame after years of abuse and abandonment by the very individuals who were supposed to protect and nurture her. For Ellen, learning how to practice self-care, decipher who is (and isn't) trustworthy, and begin to practice connection with others became the path for continued recovery and eventual emotional intimacy. Ultimately, Ellen was able to decide who she would allow into her life and with whom she would be sexual, basing her decisions on healthy factors rather than a need to self-soothe long-buried emotional trauma.

Understanding the role of emotional scarcity and how it funtions in the development of non-emotional sex as a replacement for deeper needs is vital in exploring the complexities of addictive behavior and specifically, sexually addictive behavior. No less significant in this developmental trajectory is the concept of emotional and sexual incest, both of which are examined in the following chapter.

~~~

QUESTIONS FOR YOURSELF:

- Do I become aroused by sexual conquest and disinterested after contact?

- Do I use sexual fantasy as a way to escape or numb my emotions?

- Am I only aroused by voyeuring in lieu of being sexual with a partner?

- Does my sexual contact feel like a transaction – I'll be sexual with you if…?

- Do I use sex as leverage or control over others?

- Do I use sex as a way to control my partner?

- Is anonymous sexual contact more arousing than intimate sex with my partner?

- Do I use sex as a means to exploit others?

- Do I use sex as a way to exploit my partner?

- Am I sexually aroused by situations that involve humiliation or degradation?

- Does my partner control me with sex or the promise of sex?

- Am I aroused by sex that involves risk or danger?

- In what ways do I avoid sexual contact?

QUESTIONS ABOUT YOUR PARTNER:

- Is my partner aroused by his/her need for sexual conquest?

- Does s/he use sexual fantasy as a way to escape or numb my emotions?

- Is your partner aroused by voyeuring in lieu of being sexual with you?

- Does your partner's sexual contact feel like a transaction – S/he'll be sexual if…?

- Does s/he use sex as leverage or control over your relationship?

- Does your partner use sex as a way to control you?

- Does your partner find anonymous sex more arousing than sex with you?

- Does s/he use sex as a means to exploit others?

- Dos s/he use sex as a way to exploit you?

- Is s/he sexually aroused by situations that involve humiliation or degradation?

- Does your partner control you with sex or the promise of sex?

- Is your partner aroused by sex that involves risk or danger?

- In what ways does s/he avoid sexual contact?

CHAPTER 5

FROM SCARCITY TO SURROGACY

Not all sex addicts are covert incest survivors and not all covert incest survivors are sex addicts. However, the sexual trauma of covert incest can be a virtual breeding ground for sexual addiction given the nature of the dynamics and impact on sexuality of this form of incest.

— *Ken M. Adams, Ph.D.,*
writing on Emotional Incest

Kimberly was 32 years old and struggling with commitment when she decided to seek counseling. It was in one of our early sessions that I asked about her family and, in particular, about her parents' marriage. "My parents had a good marriage. Not great, but, you know, pretty good. I know there were times that my dad wasn't happy, but you don't stay together if you're not happy, right?"

"Really? What makes you so sure?" I asked.

"Look, I saw my parents' marriage. I know that it wasn't perfect. What marriage or relationship is? My mother didn't always appreciate him, but I understood what he was really all about. There were times that he probably wanted to leave. We would talk about it because I'm the one who saw how exasperating their marriage could be. I gave him a perspective on things that no one else did. At times, he was very lonely. But he always felt so much better after we spoke. We had that special bond between us. My older brother and younger sister didn't get him, but I did. They were too busy being kids."

After a few more sessions it was clear to me that how Kimberly viewed her father was cloaked in a seductive fantasy of his love and adoration – a fantasy that would be a therapeutic challenge to explore and delicately reframe. Kimberly was already experiencing long-standing consequences of the "emotional privilege" her father "shared" with her. She just wasn't yet aware of that, let alone the fact that the privilege her father bestowed upon her was really a forced and very unhealthy imposition. And that imposition was clearly playing out in her adult relationships, as she constantly doubted her many partners' attributes, despite verbalizing her love for them. She stated in our sessions that she felt suffocated by their affection, but nonetheless chose to date. She became involved with men on a regular basis, and on two separate occasions became engaged, only to suddenly break off the engagements.

WHAT IS EMOTIONAL INCEST AND COVERT SEXUAL ABUSE?

After working with Kimberly and many other clients like her, I know that the seduction of being the "special one" is a hard nut to crack. If you're reading this chapter and the contents resonate for you, then the challenge will be in breaking through the denial and illusion that your parent's "special, just for you" love and attention was healthy and nurturing when in fact it was more likely destructive and emotionally demanding. Simply put, in a healthy parent-child relationship the child is not utilized to meet the emotional needs of the parent. Nor is there ever an inappropriate display of sexually charged emotion toward a child (even if that sexual charge is never physically acted upon). This emotional dependency of a parent upon a child is known as emotional incest, and the existence of sexually charged emotions is known as covert sexual abuse. And I can tell you after years of experience working with clients who've been subjected to one or both that emotional incest and covert sexual abuse are just as destructive as more overt forms of incest and sexual abuse. It is a long held belief that without direct sexual contact no harm is done. That belief is wrong.

Overt incest and sexual abuse is *direct sexual contact and exploitation* of a dependent person/victim by caregivers or authority figures. A child experiencing overt sexual abuse often feels trapped and used. Depending on the nature of the abuse and by whom the abuse was perpetrated, a child may also experience shame and fear.

By contrast, emotional incest and covert sexual abuse involve *the indirect yet sexualized, emotionally inappropriate abuse* of a child or dependent. No physical boundaries are crossed and no direct sexual contact is perpetrated, but a parent willingly enlists the emotional support of the child in meeting his/her otherwise unmet adult needs – a situation that may or may not become sexualized. In turn, the child becomes the confidant or emotional spouse of a same-sex or opposite-sex parent.

This inverted parent-child dynamic can exist even within a seemingly functional family where there is no obvious presence of addiction. In a stressful marriage, a physically or emotionally absent spouse can place a significant measure of dependency upon a child to fulfill the role that he or she is not filling. If, for example, you were raised in a single-parent family or in a family where one of your parents was consistently unavailable, either parent may have solicited your emotional support. This placed on you a burden of meeting that parent's adult relational needs. Further complicating this inverted relationship, there was probably a measure of sexual tension, wherein you were drawn into inappropriate discussions regarding a parent's extramarital liaisons or sexual addiction (or any number of other sexualized discussions). In this way inappropriate emotional and sexual information was shared with you as a child.

As a marriage and/or family dynamic continues to unravel, the dependency upon a child increases. The already breached boundary between parental caregiver/nurturer/protector and child is further obliterated, and the child becomes the de facto caregiver, nurturer, and protector of the parent. What ensues is the adult's engagement of the child as a way to meet the adult's emotional needs – a role that no child is capable of fulfilling, even though he or she might feel special or privileged in being relied upon in this way. Clearly in this dynamic the child is being covertly emotionally abandoned by the parent(s) and, in the process, robbed of her or his childhood.

The primary difference between overt and covert abuse is that the "privilege" of being overtly sexually abused carries an instinctive and unavoidable sense of danger, fear, and shame that is not automatically (or even usually) present with covert sexual abuse or emotional incest. In Kimberly's case, at the age of 32, she was not aware of or outwardly troubled by the burden of being her father's intimate other, despite the fact that it was unconsciously driving her away from healthy adult intimacy. In other words, her imbued family role of confidant still held self-perceived prestige and power.

EMOTIONAL AND SEXUAL TRAJECTORIES

Covert sexual abuse and emotional incest are devastating thanks largely to the indirect and insidious nature of the abuse. Adult manifestations of childhood emotional incest and/or covert sexual abuse may include:

- Codependent behavior (inappropriate boundaries or no boundaries at all)

- Guilt about practicing self-care, especially where the offending parent is concerned (an unrealistic sense of obligation to that parent)

- Difficulties related to sexual identity or gender

- Feelings of inadequacy

- Love/hate relationship with the offending parent

- Difficulty in maintaining adult relationships

- Idealization and/or devaluation of others

- Inappropriate expectations placed on partners

- Compulsivity/addiction with sex, substances, alcohol, work, food, etc.

- Patterns of triangulation (indirect communication) in work, family, or romantic relationships

- Patterns of sexual avoidance in relationships

- Patterns of compulsive sexual behavior in relationships

- Patterns of compulsive romantic attraction or a series of romantic relationships

Kimberly experiences several of these symptoms. In particular she expressed feelings of guilt about honoring her own wants and needs in her current relationship. What was apparent is that she had not yet identified the anger that was bubbling below the surface and creating a perpetual psychological impasse, in that all of her adult relationships were a no-win situation in which someone was going to be betrayed. Even her "initial" life relationship was subject to this, in that in order to find relief either she or her father would have to be betrayed. If she continued to honor her father's needs she would betray herself. And if she honored her own needs she would betray her father.

Clients like Kimberly always carry the burden of this emotional impasse. Once they identify their anger for what it is, they have the further burden of addressing it and making a decision to choose one "life" over another. In childhood Kimberly had learned to disavow her own self so she could be emotionally present for her father during his marital crises. Her father's inappropriate attachment style carried over to her and later began to surface in her romantic pursuits. Now, in therapy, she had to make a decision: Will I be true to my father, or myself?

THE WAY OUT OF THE FUNHOUSE

As with most individuals struggling with unresolved emotional incest, Kimberly's therapy began by looking at several key issues centering on a false sense of who she had become and how to connect to who she could be. Not surprisingly these areas of focus in therapy are difficult and provoke a fair amount of anxiety.

In your family of origin, identify the particular family dynamics involved.

- Recognize any patterns of emotional incest between your caregivers and you.

- Learn to set boundaries with that parent. If your caregiver is deceased, work with a therapist who can facilitate empty chair work or another experientially based modality for grief and loss.

- Acknowledge any feelings of abandonment you may have as a result of the emotional incest.

- Work toward individuation and separation from the incestuous parent by learning to take care of your abandoned-child-self.

- Working through unresolved covert abuse and journeying from wounded child to healthy adult does not have to occur in isolation if one is already involved in a committed relationship. I often encourage my clients to observe their old patterns of thought and behavior by way of their relationship in what I call a "living lab." An individual can gain a lot from observing himself/herself in the process of romantic interaction. Working with the issues as they occur in the moment is a great way to gain insight into the past. Furthermore, the sharing of one's experiences in a twelve-step support group or in a group therapy setting can be mutually healing for everyone present. Seen through the lens of Kimberly's journey, another abused individual can also attain self-awareness, emancipation, and self-empowerment.

Recently, I gave a presentation titled "Emotional Incest: The Elephant in the Therapeutic Room" at a behavioral health conference. The audience was comprised of marriage and family therapists, child therapists, social workers, psychologists, and other individuals who had heard about the lecture. This was not the first time that I had spoken on covert sexual abuse and emotional incest, and what took place after my presentation was similar to what transpired on previous occasions. Several participants approached me to share their personal stories and insights. The professionals who approached me spoke about what they were failing to recognize in some of their cases. The nonprofessionals who approached me expressed relief in finally understanding what had been previously unnamed and therefore unaddressed in their lives.

In the absence of therapy (or appropriate therapy) most individuals continue to struggle with the developmental trajectory begun by emotional incest and covert sexual abuse, all the while remaining un-aware of the problem and its origins. Often these issues remain unad-dressed because people are unaware of this dynamic until they have experienced sufficient escalation and impairment in their adult sexual and/or romantic relationships or in circumstances related to money and work, anger outbursts toward a parent or loved one, or parental trian-gulation that becomes overwhelmingly debilitating. Sometimes these symptoms manifest as eroticized rage, a concept explored in the follow-ing chapter.

~~~

QUESTIONS FOR YOURSELF:

- What was the relationship like between my mother, fa-ther or caregivers?

- Was I caught in the middle or needed to referee in their arguments?

- Do I feel a sense of fear, shame, guilt or obligation when I stand up for myself?

- If I stand up for myself do I feel as if I am abandoning my parent?

- Do I feel as if I am betraying a parent when I stand up for my spouse/partner?

- Do I feel guilt or shame when setting boundaries?

QUESTIONS ABOUT YOUR PARTNER:

- What was the relationship like between your partner's mother, father or caregivers?

- Was s/he caught in the middle or needed to referee in their arguments?

- Does your partner feel a sense of fear, shame, guilt or obligation when s/he stands up for you?

- If s/he stands up for you does your partner feel as if s/he is abandoning their parent?

- Does your partner struggle to stand up for you?

- Is your partner shamed by their parent for standing up for you?

- Does s/he feel guilt or shame when setting boundaries with their parent?

CHAPTER 6
EROTICIZED RAGE

Carl Jung: Tell me about the first time you can remember being beaten by your father.

Sabina Spielrein: It's possible...I was four. I'd broken a plate or...yes, and he told me to go into the little room and take my clothes off and then he came in and...spanked me! And then I was so frightened I wet myself...and then he hit me again! And then...
Carl Jung: That first time, how did you feel about what was happening?

[Sabina answers very quietly]
Would you repeat that? I couldn't quite hear.

Sabina Spielrein: I liked it. It excited me!

Carl Jung: And did you continue to like it?

Sabina Spielrein: Yes! Yes! Before long...he just had to say to me to go to the little room and I would...I would

start to get wet. He would just threaten, it was enough!
I'd have to go down and lie down and...and touch myself.
He would scold and it would set it off! Any kind of hu-
miliation, I looked for any humiliation! Even here, you...
you hit my...my coat with your stick, I had to come back
right away. I was so...excited! There's no hope for me.
I'm wild and filthy and corrupt. I must never be let out
of here.

— Dialogue from A Dangerous Method

It is a fact that many who struggle with sexual addiction both wittingly and unwittingly reenact shame and unresolved childhood trauma and neglect. For these individuals, shame can be synonymous with the trauma of early childhood abuse.

There are two basic types of childhood abuse. *Abuse by commission* is direct, overt, and communicated. Examples of abuse by commission are physical, sexual, and verbal abuse. Growing up in an environment with overt and direct messages that convey contempt, disapproval, dislike, and a "less than" stance results in a sense of defectiveness or broken-ness.

Conversely, *abuse by omission* is abuse conveyed by way of childhood neglect and abandonment. Infants and children (not to mention young adults) are egocentric. Humans are wired this way. Thus, our caregivers must attend to our needs and attune to our very being. Interestingly, we are the only mammals on the planet who need caregiving well into our formative years. Unfortunately, when the family system neither attunes nor attends to our needs, we experience neglect or abandonment. Being wired as egocentric, a child cannot reason that his or her needs are unmet due to extenuating and external circumstances. Instead, the child will make sense of this neglect by deciding it justified because he or she is defective, worthless, or unlovable. These shame messages, when repeated over time, feed the child's core belief system.

Though the child's early traumas may be out of sight because they are not overt, they are not easily forgotten.

Bessel van der Kolk wrote, "Many traumatized people expose themselves, seemingly compulsively, to situations reminiscent of the original trauma. These behavioral reenactments are rarely consciously understood to be related to earlier life experiences. This 'repetition compulsion' has received surprisingly little systematic exploration during the 70 years since its discovery, though it is regularly described in the clinical literature."[1] But what happens when our natural shame – that human emotion that helps us decipher humanity versus humiliation – becomes sexually charged and fused with rage? And how does that shame become sexualized in the first place? In Chapter Four, "Emotional Scarcity-Sexual Surplus" we explored Ellen's sexualized anger and her reenactment of eroticized rage in the Arousal Template. Let us now take a look at Lou Ann's story.

TOXIC SHAME

Lou Ann was only 6 years old when she first stumbled upon her father's pornographic magazines buried under the sofa cushions. Many years later, as Lou Ann sat in my office with her head hung low to her chest, she averted her eyes to avoid mine. "I am ashamed to say that I never told anyone about the magazines. I looked at them and when I was done I put them back under the cushions so that no one would know that I found them. I guess I was embarrassed that anyone would know that I saw them." Of course, as a child Lou Ann's greatest joy was making forts out of sofa cushions in her living room, so it is likely her father understood she was likely to see them. Lou Ann told me that she often "stole a peek" at the various pictures of men and women doing things that looked "weird and dirty." She recounted in therapy that the magazines portrayed women in humiliating and submissive sexual positions.

A few years later, when Lou Ann was 10, her family bought a computer. One day after school she came home and found images on the computer screen that her father had left behind. "I stared at the screen and I remembered what it was like when I would stare at the magazine pictures. I felt horny. I couldn't believe it! So I went to my room and started touching myself like I did back when I looked at my father's magazines. I was so embarrassed. It felt weird and I felt dirty. After that I couldn't stand to look my father in the eyes."

Toxic shame is caused by abuse and speaks to a pervasive sense of being flawed, defective, and worthless. It is understood this way; one doesn't *make* a mistake, one *is* a mistake. Abuse in this case was perpetrated by Lou Ann's father intentionally (though if confronted he might argue to the contrary) exposing her to inappropriate, explicit sexual images of women being sexually degraded. Lou Ann's embarrassment about finding and reading the sexually graphic material caused her to experience shame. She was quite young when she first experienced the mix of shame and arousal caused by the sexual images, and she was mostly unaware of the impact until she later stumbled upon the (intentionally?) overlooked computer images. Her buried shame came forward, only now that sexual arousal and shame became intimately fused. Her anger at her father and her sexual shame became eroticized fury or eroticized rage.

EROTICIZED RAGE

We can understand eroticized rage as sexual behaviors that fuse shame and rage and heighten sexual perversion with covert or overt levels of violence. The sexual exploration between what was considered socially normal and/or perverse was first published in 1975, by Dr. Robert Stoller, in his book, "Perversion: The Erotic Form of Hatred." Dr. Carnes later expanded on Stoller's research of sexual hatred in what he referred to as eroticized rage. "Currently, eroticized rage has been used as a term to describe the anger that is underneath sexual behavior that is socially unacceptable."[2] According to Carnes the sources of eroticized anger almost always include some of the following unresolved difficulties: grievance – revenge, resentment or entitlement, sexual, physical and emotional abuse; personality issues and self-absorbed traits of narcissism; and vulnerability – arousal that is heightened by the vulnerability of oneself or another.

All too often the shame created by childhood abuse creates a defensive shield. Usually that shield is anger. Unfortunately, anger can become "weaponized." For instance, in unhealthy and violent family systems a parent's disowned shame and guilt are easily triggered, and the result often becomes a defensive and violent reprisal (to cover or to ward off the parent's shame). This defense against a triggered sense of being "less-than" and "not-good-enough" becomes the defense of intense anger or rage, and, if history is repeated often enough, a child learns to closely associate the two.

This defensive protection against shame is in many cases intergenerational, communicated by and passed down from parents to their children with words and actions. Sometimes, when circumstances are right, as is the case with Lou Ann, discussed above, that shame turned to anger turned to rage can become sexualized. This is known as "eroticized rage."

FIT TO BE TIED

In the 2011 film, *A Dangerous Method*, Sabina Spielrein is a patient (skillfully played by the actress Keira Knightley) in a psychiatric hospital in Zurich, Switzerland. Upon her arrival at the hospital she is diagnosed with a case of hysteria and she begins treatment with the preeminent psychoanalyst, Carl Jung. Eventually we learn that Sabina's condition was triggered by the enduring humiliation and sexual arousal she felt as a child. Sex, shame and anger were fused as a result of her father's rage and his spanking Sabina while she was naked.

Shame that is caused by neglect or overt trauma may lie dormant for years before it surfaces in untold and elaborate ways. In violent family systems or in those that contain no sexual boundaries or at best reveal dysfunctional sexual boundaries and behaviors, sex becomes ensnared and inextricably twisted. As was the case with Sabina Spielrein's sexual abuse, she developed an eroticized form of adult sexual expression. This, too, occurred with Lou Ann.

Unsurprisingly, as an adult Lou Ann found it difficult to be sexually vulnerable in her romantic relationships. She reported that she needed her partners to engage in a mutual dialogue that included verbal denigration and physical restriction verging on abuse. She would insist that her partners escalate their verbal and physical cruelty, but eventually even that was not enough. Over time, Lou Ann's patterns of arousal involved her need to be bound and tied until she climaxed. Soon after the sexual exchange she became deeply ashamed and she would withdraw from her partner for days. Over time her behavior became alarming not only to her, but to those with whom she was sexual. This, according to Lee Ann, forced her to find new partners who would indulge her sexual proclivities until they too were unnerved by her requests and moved along.

When Lou Ann finally sought therapy with me she was intensely involved in the BDSM community, but she was unhappy with her need for escalating levels of abuse. With the help of therapy, Lou Ann began to understand how her early experiences were traumatic and directly related to her sexuality and sexual expression. Over time she accepted that sexual gratification and pleasure are natural and healthy.

As a result of her childhood experiences Lou Ann's adult sexual preferences were outside the realm of what most people would see as normal sexual expression. However, she learned to identify the difference between unhealthy traumatic reenactment and healthy sexual behavior that was a bit more intense. It was important for Lou Ann that she understood she could hold onto her sexual desires while healing the shameful behaviors that pervaded her early sexual development. And our continued work together helped her unveil the roots of her shame and how it manifested during sexual intimacy. Eventually her need to be abused during sex diminished to a level she was comfortable with, though it did not ever disappear entirely. More importantly, Lou Ann became willing to hold her father accountable for the abuse he perpe-trated by exposing her to sexual content at such an early age.

FRANK'S STORY REVISITED

You may remember Frank from Chapter Four, the prominent and ambitious CEO who was adamant that he didn't have a problem, even though he was regularly engaging in bisexual activity and anonymous public sex, and had nearly been arrested for indecent exposure. I had found it was unusual that in our one session he flatly stated that a loss of his career would be "a loss equal to none." It was fear of that, rather than fear of familial reprisals, that had driven Frank to call me in the first place, though by the time our appointment rolled around the terror of his near-arrest had subsided and he was back to acting out as usual.

As expected, Frank left our initial counseling session unmotivated to make changes, and he did not make another appointment – that is, until several months later when he was violently assaulted during an anony-mous sexual hook-up. His injuries were so severe that he spent sever-al days in the hospital. While he was hospitalized his wife demanded to know the truth. Slowly Frank divulged to his wife what occurred and disclosed the extent of his addiction that he had been hiding. When Frank called for an appointment a new man was on the other end of the phone.

This time around the "Frank" who appeared in my office was stripped of his former verbosity and arrogance. He told me that he had been hospitalized for injuries and then transferred to inpatient treatment for depression, alcohol and substance abuse, and sexual addiction. He'd spent the better part of seven inpatient weeks fighting what he so vi-ciously resisted – the reality that he really did have a problem and that he was a sex addict. Over the course of many months, Frank slowly and courageously became aware of the internalized shame that fueled his self-annihilating eroticized rage.

In confronting his inner demons, Frank accepted that as a child he and his brothers frequently witnessed arguments between his mother and father wherein his mother emotionally berated his father. Frank began to understand that his father had rarely (if ever) stood up to this verbal and emasculating onslaught. For years Frank hid in his upstairs bedroom and swore to himself that he would never be as weak a man as his father was in those moments. As a result of his inpatient therapy he became willing to take off his long-nurtured shield of invulnerability long enough to see that he'd turned his father's shame and pain into his own outward and inward self-denigrating sexual punishment.

Frank and I continued the work he began while in inpatient and we continued to process the grief, shame, and pain that drove his self-loathing patterns of eroticized rage. Over time he developed solid sexual sobriety, rebuilding his life in numerous ways and finding a heretofore inexperienced bond with his loving wife. His life is not perfect. As always with recovery it is progress; not perfection, but it is infinitely better and more fulfilling than it was prior to entering treatment. He now says that being violently attacked was the best thing that ever happened to him.

~~~

QUESTIONS FOR YOURSELF:

- Do I feel shame about my sexual behavior?

- Do I prefer sexual activities that are degrading and humiliating to myself?

- Do I need to increase the level of intensity or pain to myself or my partner in order to become aroused?

- Do I feel as if my sexual preferences are unhealthy or have become unhealthy?

- Do my sexual activities involve retaliation or revenge?

QUESTIONS ABOUT YOUR PARTNER:

- Do you feel shame about your partner's sexual behavior?

- Does your partner prefer sexual activities that are degrading and humiliating to her or himself?

- Does your partner need to increase the level of intensity or pain in order to become aroused?

- Do you feel as if your partner's sexual preferences are unhealthy or have become unhealthy?

- Do your partner's sexual activities involve retaliation or revenge?

PART II:

SEX, MONEY, AND POWER

Through money or power you cannot solve all problems. The problem in the human heart must be solved first.

— Dalai Lama

The confluence of sex, money and power is as eminently and persistently relevant today as it has been throughout history. The two have been partners in crime dating as far back as 1800 B.C., to ancient Babylonia. For instance, the exploits of Gilgamesh, The King of Uruk, begin in Chapter One, "The Whore of Babylon."[1] This dynamic duo showed up again for the biblical King Solomon. He may have had the dubious honor of being the world's wisest and wealthiest king and yet as the story is retold; "He threw it all away for the love of money, the pleasures of sex, and the powers of an earthly kingdom."[2] In the story of King Solomon we may see both the true greatness and the tragic failure of our own humanity – from pious devotion to self-serving gluttony.

The exploits of Gilgamesh and King Solomon are strewn across our modern day media headlines with notorious examples of the political, powerful and wealthy who gained sexual notoriety, often to their own detriment. Few, if any of us can forget how power and sex helped create ruinous desire for former President Bill Clinton; former New York state Attorney General-turned-Governor – Elliot Spitzer (as I write this book, Spitzer is attempting a political comeback in a race for New York City Comptroller), and the list goes on.

Stories from the boardrooms on Wall Street are not without their day in the sexual sun. An article published in August 2012 in the online Wall Street Journal, "a New York-based dominatrix who goes by the name of Nina Payne said she receives many visits from bankers, traders and hedge fund managers. She believes it is because they "need to take a vacation" from their "alpha-male" selves and have someone else tell them what to do, for a change."[3] Sex scandals have severely damaged countless reputations and relationships. As Henry Kissinger once said, "Power is the great aphrodisiac."

Of course, one doesn't have to be a therapist to see firsthand how the intersection of power and control by way of sex and money plays out in relationships. Off Wall Street and outside of politics there is evidence of this power interplay heard everywhere; in coffee shops, on playgrounds, in chat-rooms, in family law practices, on internet hookup websites and apps, in gyms, in self-help twelve-step meetings, and around dinner tables across the land.

For me, my time on Wall Street brought the point home and my time in therapy as a client and now as a therapist has merely reinforced the idea. Sex, money and power are as intermingled as ever, in as many infinite variations as power and control or human incentive will devise. Consider the following:

- A wife turns a blind eye to her husband's ongoing marital indiscretions in order to maintain her lifestyle.

- Men and women pay for sexual services outside of their primary relationship.

- A spouse keeps a secret bank account or stash of funds "just in case."

- A cheating husband accumulates credit card debt to appease his wife and assuage his own guilt for his furtive sexual betrayal.

- A spouse secretly gambles with the children's college fund and incrementally loses it all.

- Jewelry and other material items are knowingly given and accepted as an apology for infidelity in a relationship.

The common thread in all of these situations is some form of hubris and power differential – created by age, income level, looks, social standing, intellect, etc. Show me a relationship that is laden with sexual and financial exploitation and I'll show you two people who struggle with a disparity of power and core messages of worthlessness. On the inside, safely locked away from knowing eyes (including one's own, sometimes), is their lack of trust and safety with themselves and their partner.

DOWN THE RABBIT HOLE

At our core is often an unspoken and sometimes commanding influential grab for power and control. In marriage or romantic relationships in which money becomes a primary factor in establishing and maintaining equality (or inequality), the spoils of "conflict" couldn't be steeper.

The case of Gail and Brad provides an excellent example. Gail had shepherded Brad into therapy on the premise that she wanted them to learn how to communicate better. Once in my office, where Gail presumed Brad was less than likely to run from confrontation, she professed how lonely she was in the relationship, as well as how fed up she was becoming with Brad's excessive work schedule. Since Brad was apparently not willing to reduce his work hours and spend more quality time with her, she vowed to stop having sex with him until they "learned to communicate."

In Gail's mind "communication" meant "I'll tell you what I don't like about you and you'll listen." Her moratorium on sex was nothing more than a thinly veiled retaliation against Brad's avoidance of intimacy. In Brad's world "communication" translated to "We're here again? We're having this argument again? OK, fine. I'll avoid you and stay distracted with work or with alcohol, porn and emotional affairs." In our initial session, I began to think about my work with Adam (Part 1 "Sex, Love and Longing"). Adam was reluctant to revisit his childhood experiences; however, he stuck with therapy and eventually understood why he ran from his relationships; he experienced emotional neglect in his childhood and had a negative self-worth. Money, in lieu of affection, was a substitute for love and attention.

Adam and Brad's story might sound similar. Adam exits the relationship when his anxiety becomes overwhelming and Brad exits his relationship during conflict. And they both turn to alcohol, pornography and a wall of silence in turmoil. But that's where the similarities end and the differences begin for the underlying forces that compel both men's behavior.

Let us review for a moment. Those with a fearful-avoidant attachment style, like Adam, rely on others to maintain a positive self-view which in turn sets them up to become dependent on their partner although they are very hesitant to get attached. Adam struggled in his relationships because of his fear of being abandoned by his partner and believed that women were only attracted to him because of his financial worth rather than the love and connection he might bring to the equation. His negative self-talk was quick to remind him that, "it was only a matter of time before these women wised up and saw me for the inadequate man I am."

Brad has a dismissive attachment style which means that he and others like him covet their autonomy above all else. He exudes a seductive manner that conveys interest but does not allow for deeper emotional and relational connection. Pia Mellody refers to this as a wall of seduction. I refer to this seduction as "peacock strutting."

According to Gail, when she and Brad first started dating and even into the early years of their marriage, Brad was attentive and spent most of his free time with Gail. Brad even concurred that he was attracted to Gail and had hoped to catch her attention. But Gail was quick to point out that this all changed in short order. "I woke up one day and realized that I was married to a different man. I thought we were still emotionally connected." But as Gail stated, "He was in the early stage of his ongoing love affair with work."

When we first met Brad had no intention of staying in therapy. He rejected Gail's concerns rather than trying to understand them and went so far as to insinuate that she had little to complain about since Brad's efforts and hard-earned money afforded her a lifestyle that was hard to criticize! He later acknowledged that the only reason he came to therapy at all was to pacify *his wife*. But during that initial session and in spite of his efforts to convey otherwise I caught a glimpse of an emotional tenderness that he kept hidden and protected by layers of sarcasm.

"Where did you learn to be so independent and invulnerable," I asked?

"I don't know," he said. "I've always been independent. It's what made me who I am today. What? Are you going to tell me that there's something wrong with that?"

"There's nothing wrong with that," I said. "I'm just curious."

"About?"

"About that young boy turned young man with a sweet heart and a biting sarcasm, that's all?"

In our initial session I asked Brad to consider therapy for a short stint in order to explore his obvious need to flee intimacy. Brad begged off therapy citing his unpredictable and overbooked schedule, but I knew how to spin this as an investment opportunity.

"Brad, look – the time and money you spend on your own personal therapy will serve to reap personal and professional rewards for you, tenfold. The cost/benefit of that deal is so low risk – high reward that I'd take that deal *all day, every day*. I knew that he placed a value on financial success and independence – this was a no brainer. The question for me was how to help Brad see therapy as an opportunity not a punishment.

Brad did decide to show up for therapy, in fact, weekly. Months later, when he was still working on identifying his emotions and the ways in which he retreated into and exploited Gail from his proverbial foxhole, he turned to me in genuine oblivion and said, "This relationship stuff is hard! You mean to say that I have to work at it every day?" "No," I said, "Only if you want it to succeed."

People, like Brad, with a dismissive attachment style, learn early in life that showing vulnerability is unacceptable. In our sessions Brad began to lower his strong impervious façade. On one occasion he admitted that he really liked coming to therapy although he couldn't elaborate why. Brad's emotional invulnerability had always served him well. He leaned on money, control and power to feel good about himself and his early life success and approval from his father was honed by his ability to prove his financial prowess. There wasn't much room for vulnerability when his father prided stoicism and drive above all else.

I recognized that Brad didn't reveal his vulnerability to too many people so I was particularly touched when, during a difficult but insightful session, he paused and said, "It's kind of hard [to trust] when no one was there for me and I had to fend for myself. It was both terrifying but really clear that I had no choice *but* to be strong."

In therapy the question of, "Why therapy," Or, "Why now?" serves as an early launch point in the process. Most aspects of my work with Brad were unusual. Despite his protective shield, he was willing to be vulnerable. Despite his predisposition for avoidance he chose the connection of therapy and in spite of his lack of interest to participate in the first place, he stayed. Brad eventually finished therapy as many often do…happier and having found what they came looking for. In Brad's case I was never really sure what he wanted out of it except a way to be more personally and professionally successful. After all, that was the bait.

Some clients close out therapy with an acknowledgement that they are "good for now." Others stop coming or withdraw without fanfare or notice. I would have thought that Brad would be one of the clients who saunter off without so much as a parting phone call or cancelled session; but I was wrong. Brad showed for his appointment and announced that he "now has a new appreciation for his life," and wanted to end therapy. He exorcised his hidden demons and voiced why he chose work and money over his wife and kids. "It's all I knew; all that I learned growing up. As long as I brought home money or something to contribute to the household expenses I had a right to be in the family." Brad asked for but never needed an open invitation to return for a seat on the couch should he ever want to come back.

Whether or not Brad would continue to work at emotional intimacy with Gail was yet to be determined. Could or would Brad continue to place a value on connection over autonomy or love over labor? Compared to the many men I typically see he was an anomaly because most of the men who come to therapy do so by force or by foul. Brad was willing to stay (albeit not at first) in order to better understand himself.

As we'll explore in Part Two, loosening the grip on money, sex or power involves first exploring the ways in which its influence is wielded.

~~~

QUESTIONS FOR YOURSELF:

- Do I choose autonomy over connection in a relationship?

- What don't I want others to know about me?

- What don't I like about how I relate to myself or others?

- What would I most like to change about myself?

- What does communication mean to me?

- When I speak with my partner am I respectful?

QUESTIONS ABOUT YOUR PARTNER:

- Does my partner choose connection or distance in a relationship?

- Does my partner accept me for who I am?

- Is my partner authentic about who he is?

- What does communication mean to my partner?

- Is my partner respectful in communication?

CHAPTER 7
ICARUS REVISITED

An inflated consciousness is always egocentric and conscious of nothing but its own existence. It is incapable of learning from the past, incapable of understanding contemporary events, and incapable of drawing right conclusions about the future. It is hypnotized by itself and therefore cannot be argued with. It inevitably dooms itself to calamities that must strike it dead.

— Dr. Carl Jung

My years of experience on Wall Street introduced me to a wealth of men who engaged in power grabbing behaviors and impression management. (Greater numbers of women eventually climbed their way to loftier bastions of power but that wasn't until a decade or so later.) In the late 80s and 90s, investment banks were brimming with legions of young, hawkeyed traders and bankers riding the crest of financial excess and glory. The stories of men who enjoyed a meteoric rise to professional and personal heights, only to then plunge into a financial and personal crash and burn (known as a "blow-out"), were legendary. Some men saw their "fall from grace" as a painful summons to a deeper, more introspective place, yet many more continued to addictively pursue the never-ending cycle of self-destructive behaviors – financial shenanigans, moral superiority, and sexual excess – while remaining oblivious to the inevitable; refusing to believe their shameless monetary and sexual escalation would once again inevitably lead to collapse. And as they repeated this self-destructive downward spiral one could only postulate what fueled their never ending pursuit of all things gluttonous. In the recovery field we refer to this as "the definition of insanity: *doing the same things over and over and expecting different results.*"

It was on Wall Street that I first became aware of individuals who were blindly driven by an inner compulsion for success and excess. I still think about the multiplicity of men in the financial arena who were determined, nay obsessed, by dominance, hungry men with a need for power, achievement, and praise from on high. They, like me before recovery, had no concept or understanding of the psychological confluence of childhood events that may lead an individual to this deep-seated need for approval and success – in spite of their morals, values, and everything else they deemed important.

As a therapist I have sat with many emotionally disconnected males. Oftentimes in our sessions their primary albeit unconscious goal is to deflect my therapeutic gaze. I have come to see my time with them as an opportunity for my own professional growth and a means to hold the proverbial emotional floor as the client weaves his reality into that which ultimately preserves his self-concept. Given that their narcissistic wounding neither often allows for inward reflection nor for others to truly know them, the emotional burden of seeing the light defaults to those entwined in their relational webs of manipulation and their deceptive interpretations of reality.

When taken to an extreme, this behavior is captured in the phenomenon called gaslighting. The term was derived from the 1938 play *Gas Light* and the subsequent, 1944 film adaptation of the same name, starring Ingrid Bergman. This mystery-thriller helped forge the expression that describes psychological abuse in which the abuser presents information with the intent of making a victim doubt his or her own memory, perception and sanity. Instances range from simple denial of wrongdoing by a partner to more severe disorienting of another's reality.

For many narcissists and addicts alike, the need for psychological self-preservation comes at the expense of a loved one's vulnerability.

MIRROR, MIRROR, ON THE WALL

A fall from grace brings to mind one particular client, named Joe. As he sat across from me in our first session I couldn't help but wonder what the actual precipitating event was that brought Joe to therapy. He had told me, "My wife thinks that I have a problem," which is an all-too-common statement from many men attending therapy for sexual compulsivity. What they usually mean is, "I don't have a problem but my wife (significant other, partner) says I do so I'm seeing you as a way to appease her (them)." Or, "I don't have a problem but I'll come to therapy for a while until this whole thing blows over." Sometimes a job or career, or "the prosecutor and judge" can be substituted for the word "wife." Whatever the particular circumstances, these men nearly always arrive in treatment not because they want but because they are desperate to save something. The only question with Joe was who or what that something was.

As is often the case, Joe spent the better part of forty-five minutes nibbling around the edges of my question, "What brought you to therapy?" What I mostly got from him were the caveats: therapy had failed him in the past; other therapists didn't "get" him (present company excluded and no disrespect to me, of course); other therapists were only interested in his childhood and not in the underlying reasons for which he was seeking therapy which were, as of that moment, still unknown to me.

"Fine," I finally said. "Let's do this. What would you most like for me to know about you?" Joe sat in rapt contemplation and then, with a glance that strongly hinted at, "now we're getting somewhere," began to speak. "Well... I'm well-meaning. I work hard and I really care a lot about what people think."

I nodded. "Go on."

"I'm a good husband, but my wife keeps saying that I don't love her." I could see that he was winding up for "the pitch." "As you can probably tell...."

Here, he glanced knowingly in my direction,

"I am good at what I do and very successful. So you would think that by now she would understand that I have to work long hours. My job isn't just a 9 to 5 thing. And she should definitely realize there's no way in hell she'll continue to have the lifestyle that she demands if I'm not putting in the hours!" He took one last pause and said, "I would communicate all of that with her if she wasn't so reactive and uptight about sex. So, how's that?"

In that very moment I found an irony of association too compelling to ignore. It was as though Joe had channeled the very essence of Ari Gold, the quasi-fictional lead character in HBO's *Entourage*. (Ari Gold's character is based on the Executive Director's real-life agent with full Hollywood swagger and self-aggrandizing bravado.) Essentially, Ari is a powerful movie agent, arguably the most powerful agent in "the industry." He is obsessed with those who are not obsessed with him; he is arrogant to an extreme, but he condescendingly acquiesces to his wife's desires because she holds entrée to her family inheritance, which is ultimately what Ari covets above all else. Joe's statement that he would communicate with his wife if she wasn't so uptight about sex reminded me of an *Entourage* episode in which Ari, in his inimitable, sexist yet charming contempt, declares the reason for his coming to a therapy session: "I came here today because I thought this was a session on how my wife could learn to communicate."[1]

I was not surprised by Joe's grandiosity. As a matter of fact, it would have been shocking to hear something inherently productive like introspective reflection and a list of his goals for treatment. By their very nature, narcissists compensate with grandiosity for their struggle with insufficiency-of-self. They are disconnected from themselves in much the same way that almost all addicts are disconnected from themselves – persistently thinking they are "not good enough," at least while in the throes of their addiction.

Ari Gold and Dan Draper of *Mad Men* – to name another – are two fictional men for whom self-worship has bestowed much and delivered little. Fictional as those men may be, they are in many ways no different than the disconnected male clients who present in my practice, failing to understand their inner selves and communicate their emotions. In fact even to recognize that they have emotions is completely foreign to these men. For these individuals success is measured not by what they possess but by what they have yet to conquer. The concept of enough does not exist; *nearly* or *almost* sounds like failure; *how you see me* drives all that I do. In reality, these people operate from a core insufficiency-of-self, compensating for their insecurity by gaining power, control, and money. Their never-ending quest for external approval masks their true desire of inner fulfillment.

After his "So, how's that?" query, Joe stared at me, seeming very proud of his self-revelatory statements and waiting for, and probably expecting, my vote of approval. But he had missed the major point. Not one thing that he'd told me about himself actually allowed me to know *him*. What Joe had shared was how he viewed himself through other's eyes, and his projection of self that said, essentially, "Am I amazing, or what?"

Nonetheless, in that moment Joe told me more than he realized. Introspection is not a narcissist's strong suit, and despite his belief that he cared a lot about what others think, he was actually more concerned about what others think *of him*. These two concepts are clearly and completely different.

OF MEN AND GREEK GODS

Early childhood psychosocial dynamics can set in motion an individual's continuous and ever increasing need for external approval. Left to its natural progression, that level of self-promotion and fulfillment will ultimately fall short, necessitating a need for an even greater level of psychological reward all in an all-out effort to mask one's inner void – the core belief that one is inherently unworthy. Joe's sense of self consisted of his narcissistic reliance on a feedback loop of what others thought of him. This showed me very clearly that his self-view depended on acceptance and approval by others and that this had probably been the case since early childhood.

The stories of self-preoccupation and blind ambition, as noted earlier, are mythical and no less present in current day. People with deep narcissistic wounds and a gaping insufficiency of self are driven entirely by their obsessional focus on conquest, achievement, and adulation. American psychologist Henry A. Murray published his "Icarus Complex" theory in 1955, suggesting that human behavior is driven by an internal state of disequilibrium. "We have a LACK of something and this drives us. We are dissatisfied and we desire something."[2]
Consider the following analysis of Murray's work:

> *"The Icarus Complex is a constellation of mental conflicts, the degree of which reflects the imbalance between a person's desire for success, achievement, or material goods, and the ability to achieve those goals; the greater the gap between the idealized goal and reality, the greater the likelihood of failure."* [3]

It is worth noting that there is a fine line between pride and hubris, and finer still between hubris and self-destruction. It is natural to want approval, to be noticed, and to be thought well of. But the lines between healthy need and internal emptiness are where we find the difference.

Further to this point, let us consider two Greek myths: the stories of Narcissus and Icarus. Narcissus was a young man of unimaginable physical beauty. His physical appearance was admired by male and female alike, but he rejected their advances and was contemptuous of their admiration. Many nymphs fell in love with Narcissus; none were more obsessed than Echo, who pined for his love and devotion and spent her life waiting in vain. Echo eventually became so distraught about Narcissus' rejection that she withered and died. Several Gods drew revenge on Narcissus, cursing him to a life of pining and unfulfilled love. And so it was that Narcissus fell in love with the sight of his glorious image reflected back in a pond's shimmering water. His love and obsession for this person reflected in the pond was all-consuming, but impossible to consummate. Narcissus lay for days enraptured by his own reflection and simultaneously tortured by the realization that he could never possess the object of his infatuation. In time, Narcissus stopped eating, lost his beautiful looks, and died.

Icarus provides a similar cautionary tale about ambition and arrogance. Icarus and his father Daedalus were imprisoned inside a labyrinth that Daedalus had built for King Minos of Crete to capture the Minotaur, a half-bull, half-man creature. In an attempt to escape the labyrinth, Daedalus created two sets of wings made from feathers and wax. Before flight, Daedalus cautioned his son to follow him and at all costs to avoid flying both too close to the sun and too close to the sea. However, Icarus was overwhelmed with his ability to soar, and, instead of listening to his father's cautionary words, he flew with reckless abandon. In the process, of course, he flew too close to the sun, the sun melted the wax, and the wings fell apart. Icarus fell into the sea and drowned.

The twenty-first century versions of Narcissus and Icarus are the type-A personalities I used to see on Wall Street and that I now see on many days in my therapeutic practice. These men and women are driven by their inner compulsions for success, domination, and admiration. They operate from a sense of entitlement and false power, and they are compelled to reenact their deep psychological wounds for attention and adulation.

In many cases, people with narcissistic personality disorder:

- Tend to be self-centered or arrogant.

- Seek constant attention, approval or admiration

- Consider themselves to be better than others

- Exaggerate their talents and accomplishments

- Believe that they are entitled to special treatment

- Believe that other "special" people are worthy of attention

- Are easily hurt but may not outwardly show it

- May seek retaliation or revenge if offended

- May take advantage of others to achieve their goals

Of particular note is their preoccupation with fantasies that help them perpetuate their internal need for high praise and acceptance.

HAMARTIA

To simply label these individuals as narcissistic or addicted does not capture the full breadth of the internal psychological discrepancies that are at odds within them. Essentially, these men and women can, with outward impunity, engage in their self-protective behaviors at the expense of their authentic selves – sometimes never examining their deeper issues. And most times, it is the result of early deficits in attachment, poor ego state integration in childhood, and other unhealthy early-life family dynamics.

As previously discussed in Chapter One, "Sex, Love, and Attachment," in question here are the ways in which early childhood stressors or traumas now manifest in their lives. To act with total disregard and a lack of empathic awareness toward others requires a capacity to compartmentalize and split off the parts of self that are too loathsome to acknowledge. The split-off parts of self that carry the shame, guilt, fear, and loneliness of childhood are buried deep, hidden from the public, and masked by grandiosity and self-entitlement.

Consider for a moment one of the greatest sports figures of all time, pro golfer Tiger Woods. His celebrity had reached an almost mythic level before his life unraveled and his messy serial infidelity was revealed first to his unsuspecting wife and later to the world. Tiger's tale was a sumptuous sex scandal on which both professional and social media feasted for months. Tiger became a modern-day Narcissus and Icarus all rolled into one – high on himself and his achievements, drunk on the dizzying heights of his fame before he fell as abruptly as anyone ever has – descending all the way into mere mortality and vulnerability. Some suspect he is still trying to come to terms with this, and why not? When you've been a God, becoming a mortal is not exactly satisfying. Of course, Tiger Woods is but one sporting example of presumption of being godlike and attempting to overstep his human limitations. The Greeks called this hamartia. Mark Sanford, Gary Hart, John Edwards, and Mark Foley are but some of the names that round out a political list of twenty-first century Icarus men.

JP Morgan Chase and Co. (the biggest U.S. bank) and its current CEO, Jamie Dimon, (who ironically hails from Greece and is from a long line of Greek bankers), experienced his Icarus moment in January 2013. His firm's unbridled exposure to high-risk debt helped to contribute to the 2007 – 2012 global financial crisis and near nuclear meltdown of our nation's financial system. Of course JP Morgan was not alone in their high-flying predatory frenzy but in his January testimony to Congress, Dimon called his firm's loss of over $6 *billion* (to date one of the steepest losses ever experienced by a multinational bank), "an embarrassing mistake," and one for which he professed, "I am absolutely responsible."[4] Dimon's admissions to Congress and to his investors at JP Morgan Chase eventually cost him a fifty percent pay cut – substantial by any person's standards but one which only brought a yawn by Wall Street's. It's hard to summon sympathy when a pay cut of fifty percent results in a take-home salary of $11.5 million. Still, Jamie Dimon's penance was a mere drop in the larger U.S. economic devastation that resulted from and began with the 2008 collapse of the U.S. housing bubble and the sub-prime mortgage market – the worst economic U.S. financial crisis since the Great Depression.

The case of Bernie Madoff, financier-turned public-enemy number one, remains one for the modern day mythology books. The scandal surrounding Bernie Madoff and his wealth management business came to light in the midst of the larger financial crisis. In March, 2009, Madoff pleaded guilty to 11 federal felonies and admitted to a massive Ponzi scheme that defrauded thousands of investors out of *billions* of dollars. Madoff's investors included close family, lifelong friends, and hundreds of wealthy clients. The duration and level of moral corruption engaged in by Madoff was simply astounding, and it speaks directly to the nefarious side of dissociative compartmentalization. Consider the following: "A prison psychologist, with whom Madoff spends significant amounts of time, has told him he has been able to cope with his problems over the years by 'compartmentalizing' them, and he still does, he added." [5]

After a public scandal, some men like Tiger Woods, Anthony Weiner, Elliot Spitzer and thousands of others we've never heard of begrudgingly seek therapy or something similar to it. They may arrive as my client Joe did, insisting that they don't have a real problem. In the moments when I am sitting across from them in my office, I remind myself that the very act of speaking to a therapist probably took a great deal of courage, even if that courage was cloaked in misguided denial or contempt. I prefer to believe that on some level, even if only deep inside, they know they do have a problem, and that to overcome it they need outside help. After all, hardly anyone wakes up in the morning, feels good about him- or herself, and decides to muck it up by going into therapy. Hardly anyone wants to look, really look, at his or her dark side, to ferret out the blind spots in their mind and heart. So, for me, showing up in therapy, even if the person is the most ardent twenty-first-century Icarus male, is something I view as a de facto act of contrition.

Joe came to therapy because something upset the delicate balance of his life: in this case, his wife. To manage his stress, Joe drank but never to the point that he was unable to sustain the belief (denial) that he had a problem. He worked too much but most of the time it was to help his children (they were grown and living on their own) and he adhered to a daily morning ritual of compulsive masturbation to "clear his mind for better concentration" (accessing pornography in the ritualistic process.) Joe managed to be exquisitely in control of a very out-of-control life by compartmentalizing. But now as Joe sat in my office, he had become out of control of being in control of this delicate fragmentation. On some level his guilt, shame and denial had managed to leak like toxic sludge.

CHAPTER 8
FINANCIAL INFIDELITY

The modern conservative is engaged in one of man's oldest exercises in moral philosophy; that is, the search for a superior moral justification for selfishness.

— *John Kenneth Galbraith*

My good friends Rob Weiss and Jennifer Schneider have stated the following about infidelity: *Infidelity is the keeping of secrets in an intimate partnership.* Extending their thoughts on the matter, I define *financial infidelity* as the keeping of *financial secrets* in an intimate partnership. After years of working with partners betrayed by their spouse's financial indiscretions and infidelity, I can say with certainty that it is often just as devastating as sexual infidelity.

One such example of financial infidelity occurred between Hillary and her husband Andrew. Following a fight, Hillary called me and asked for an emergency session. She related their violent argument:

"So how come I don't know anything about this $100K?" Hillary asked.

"Of course you do, I told you all about it," Andrew said.

"You told me about $100K? Really and when did that happen?"

"If you can't remember, how should I?" Andrew was convinced that his attempts at denial could be pawned off as a slip of his wife's memory.

Hillary screamed, "Do I look stupid to you? Do I look like a fucking idiot?

I must, because I'm sure as hell being treated like one? Honestly, how the hell can you even suggest that I forgot about one-hundred thousand dollars? Oops, that's where I left my pocket change! I knew it had to be around here somewhere...Yeah, that's it, I must have forgotten about it around the same time I left the kids at the grocery store!"

At this point Hillary was utterly enraged. She advanced toward Andrew. "How...dare...you...steal...that...money...from...our...joint...account...without...my...signature! And you got that putz of a broker to cover your sorry little ass and lie for you!" Suddenly Hillary lunged at Andrew, grabbing him by the throat and heaving him against the wall.

"Do...not...ever...EVER...again steal my money and try to pass it off as my having known about it. I'm doing everything in my power to save me and the kids from bankruptcy and all you do is undermine me at every turn. If you do this again, I will choke the very life from your lungs and bring you to within one last miserable breath of your pathetic life!"

Hillary had called me in a panic and now I knew why. I was glad that I saw her that day. "I've hit my limit," she repeated. "He either leaves for treatment, or I'll divorce him immediately. Either way, I'm not sure that I want to stay married to him. I can't take it anymore! I've been living with this for too long and I've been pushed too far."

Her reference to "living with this for too long" was about the couple's marital problems as a result of Andrew's struggle with managing their business. Months earlier I had received a phone call from Hillary who detailed the reasons for which she was seeking therapy. It was clear to me that she needed individual therapy as much or more than they needed couple's counseling so I suggested that perhaps we could meet and assess the best course for therapy.

Hillary was upset about the company's mounting losses and the fact that her husband appeared unable to manage the company's finances. In one of our early sessions, she stated to me, "I said that I would be supportive of our decision to buy this company but now I'm not so sure. *Our* money is tied up in this and he just thinks I'm being critical when I say something."

My work with Hillary involved giving support, teaching her how to practice self-care and Hillary learning how to handle her husband's deteriorating state of mind. As a result of the stress he was under, Andrew appeared to be emotionally deteriorating. I was as concerned for his emotional state as I was concerned for Hillary's and it was now apparent that their marriage needed more help than individual therapy and their sporadic couple's sessions would provide.

As the weeks passed their home and work situation worsened. Hillary grew more impatient with Andrew when she tried to help him and he insisted that both he and the company were doing fine. Yet that insistence flew in the face of his increasing hostility and rancor toward Hillary which was followed by his bouts of sleeplessness and anxiety. Their tension hit a fever pitch until that day when it erupted in an all-out confrontation.

As I listened to Hillary recount the details from their personal *Saturday Night Massacre*, I cautioned her against making impulsive decisions regarding their marriage given the extreme state of their financial and marital turmoil. I also feared that Hillary's escalating rage might land her in jail or worse.

The day after I met with Hillary for her emergency session, I met with Hillary and Andrew in order to establish a safe therapeutic direction. I quickly learned what had been percolating. Andrew had been silently fighting to keep the company financially solvent. The revelation that the company was teetering on the edge of bankruptcy was, for Hillary, a new and terrifying disclosure, especially since their entire personal wealth was securing the company's very financial viability. Therefore, a bankruptcy for the company would almost certainly mean personal financial devastation as well.

This loss, however grave for Hillary, was less a concern for Andrew. He feared public scrutiny of his personal failure more than he feared personal and corporate bankruptcy. It was the threat of public exposure that motivated Andrew to try to convince Hillary that he was "fine" and didn't need treatment.

"You don't understand," he said. "This can all be fixed. I think you're being irrational."

"I'm irrational?" she yelled! His attempt to dissuade Hillary prompted me to lean forward in my chair in order to protect either one of them from spontaneous violence. Hillary vowed that she truly had enough and was now fighting for her life.

"I don't know what will become of me or my life, but I know that I can't allow this to continue. I'm giving you two choices; one: you agree to go to treatment right away or I'm filing for immediate divorce. Two: if you do not decide to go to treatment right away I'll remove you from our house until you do. I am not going to make any decisions about our marriage for now."

Faced with this threat, you'd have thought that Andrew would have signed on the dotted line, but that's the incredulity of a narcissistic wound: At all costs, the preservation of a narcissist's self-worth and esteem take precedence over all else. "I've allowed myself to be pacified, manipulated and duped one too many times. I'm done," she said.

As a therapist, I hoped that Hillary and Andrew could work through (and beyond) this latest round of financial infidelity, but I also knew that would mean months of individual and marital therapy that neither party seemed ready to endure. I wasn't sure that Andrew's narcissism could ever allow him to be authentic or honest about himself. I also questioned whether Hillary's post-traumatic stress after years of Andrew's financial deceit had eroded her self-worth so much so that she would never be able to trust Andrew again. It seemed to me that too much history and wounding had come between them, and this final grievance really was the last straw – one final insult in a long string of grievances that involved large business debt and new disclosures of financial betrayal.

Hillary and Andrew's story is only one example of financial exploitation and betrayal. The statistics actually point to a widespread national prevalence. For instance, a 2012 survey conducted by *today. com* and *Self* magazine found that nearly half of the 23,000 respondents acknowledged keeping money secrets from their partner. The survey found that forty-six percent of people had lied to their partner about money – everything from lying about or hiding purchases to clandestinely withdrawing money from joint accounts."[1] Ten percent of respondents reported keeping serious financial secrets involving secret bank accounts or hidden credit card debt. Thirteen percent reported a divorce or relational split due to this level of deception in the partnership.

Another online poll, this one conducted in 2011 by Harris Interactive for Forbes Woman and the National Endowment for Financial Education (NEFE), surveyed 2,019 U.S. adults. The leading money struggles in partnerships involved smaller indiscretions like hiding cash, minor purchases, and bills. That said, a significant number of people admitted larger issues such as hiding major purchases, keeping secret bank accounts, and lying about their debt or earnings. A closer look revealed that 58% of the participants hid cash, 54% hid a minor purchase, 30%

hid a bill, 16% hid a major purchase, 15% hid a bank account, 11% lied about debt, and 11% lied about earnings. [2]

Furthermore, sixteen percent of the respondents said that a money lie had led to a divorce, and 11% said it had led to a separation. As I mentioned earlier, financial betrayal is every bit as damaging as sexual betrayal. Sadly, the two often go hand-in-hand, doubling down on the pain that is delivered to an unsuspecting partner.

WHERE THERE'S SMOKE, THERE'S FIRE

Hillary and Andrew's marital difficulties did not include sexual infidelity, but that is not always (or even usually) the case. In fact, many betrayed spouses first encounter evidence of sexual betrayal when overlooked or discarded credit card receipts, phone bills, or work vouchers are discovered. In the early phases of betrayal there may not be any sign that a partner is withdrawing or allocating time and money toward another person, behavior, or addiction. A fluctuation in mood due to work, family, or emotional stressors is a common event in anyone's life. But, when the baseline behavior for an individual is noticeably changed for an extended period of time, the awareness of something amiss can become too strong to ignore. Mounting warning signs that something is NQR (not quite right) often leads a betrayed partner to question if something is happening in their relationship, and at this point will go to great lengths – if not any – to learn the truth. Often this results in "detective"-type behaviors – checking phones, bills, pockets, purses, expense reports, and the like – that uncover the truth (or at least part of the truth). For example:

- I knew something was different about my husband when he became quiet and more withdrawn. Then I noticed that there were cash advances drawn on our credit card, and some unexplained charges. After checking with the credit card company I confronted him about the charges. He became enraged at my insinuation that he might be doing something without my knowledge. I could only imagine that he must be having an affair and spending the money on other women. After that I started checking his phone and emails, and I found plenty of evidence showing that was exactly what he was doing.

- Our accountant called when we were preparing our tax returns and asked about interest income from a savings account. I didn't want to tell him that I didn't know anything about that account, so I deferred to my husband. That night I questioned my husband when he came home. That was the beginning of the end. He acknowledged that he was having an affair, which over time I realized were really multiple affairs.

- In the early years my wife was busy raising the kids while I was consumed with growing my business. I needed to keep up an image of success, so I spent a lot of money on country club memberships, dinners with friends. This also included expensive gifts to the different women that I was sneaking around with. She never knew how much I was spending until the money disappeared and I couldn't keep up appearances any longer. It was only when I had to file for bankruptcy that she learned about the spending, and also the sleeping around.

GOLDEN HANDSHAKES OR GOLDEN HANDCUFFS

I was curious about how the issue of financial infidelity plays out in places other than a therapist's office so I called my friend Jay R. Penney, a Certified Financial Planner to find out. I've known Jay for many years and I always enjoy his outlook about money and investing. Jay is a man whose caring personality and quiet manner never fit the dog-eat-dog insensitivity of money and investing that I came to know on Wall Street.

He sports a tall posture, deep barrel chest and a confident handshake worthy of attention. If he wasn't a money manager he could certainly pass for a diplomat. In all his years of portfolio design, and managing wealth and investments for people with deep, deep pockets (I'm sure having also come across a narcissist or two along the way) he must have encountered financial infidelity in his line of work.

"I build relationships so I spend a lot of time with families and couples getting a sense of who they are and what matters to them most. I begin with a 61-question assessment to measure risk, values, goals and relationship. The majority of investors are pretty risk averse and phobic around money. They're not usually willing to take big risks with their assets and it is important to me that I know my client's tendencies."

I remember this questionnaire. Some years ago, when I was transitioning from active day-trader to active therapist, I approached Jay about managing some of my investments. I was also no longer in a position to actively oversee my finances so I turned to Jay for help. Risk aside, I asked Jay about infidelity. He stated that he had several clients who arranged their postnuptial agreements to include vesting schedules for years of matrimonial service. One such couple came to mind.

"I had a very affluent divorced client who became quite an eligible bachelor. After dating a woman for some months he proposed to her: a successful business woman in her own right and twenty-five years his junior."

According to Jay, the caveat in his proposal was that she quit her job in order to accompany him when he travels. Being the businesswoman that she was, Jay alleged, she told him that she would quit her lucrative job in order to travel with him *but* she wanted remuneration. "She negotiated a comfortable compensation package, complete with vesting schedule for time served. She'll never be primary beneficiary of the estate," he said, "But she'll be paid handsomely."

"I don't know about you, Jay, but that sounds to me like a well-compensated albeit high-priced escort." Jay remained silent – although I could swear that I heard him smile.

The notion of payment for job termination, known as a Golden Parachute, reportedly dates back to 1961 when creditors allegedly tried to oust Howard Hughes from his control of the now defunct Trans World Airlines. In similar fashion, a golden handshake is a bonus when you take a new position. The prenuptial agreement negotiated between Jay's client and his girlfriend was actually a combination of the two, though it sounded to me more like a set of golden handcuffs than anything else. Sex for money by any name isn't necessarily infidelity. It's an exchange of currency. But my initial question about financial infidelity was still out there.

"From time to time, I come across a situation upon a family member's or individual's death that exposed an undeclared bank account or asset. However, those situations are far and few in-between."

This prompted Jay to recall an unusual story.

"Some years back I received a call from a recently widowed client who discovered that her husband had left a note in his will. In this letter he disclosed that he had buried large quantities of precious metal ingots on property that he had secretly purchased several states away for the sole purpose of hiding the treasure. Her worries were two-fold: where on the vast property was the treasure buried and would the IRS hold her accountable for back taxes and penalties?"

What did she do," I asked? I was all in. I'm all about modern day treasure hunts!

"Well, I called a colleague who is a forensic accountant and put them in contact. Then I arranged for retrieval, appraisal, and sale of the ingots. The widow did not go there herself so we had a family member represent her and oversee the transaction. It was pretty exciting. We didn't really know what we would find since she had no idea that the property nor the ingots existed." This infidelity it seemed turned out to be quite rewarding for her.

I asked why Jay supposed that the widow's deceased husband might have done this. He ventured to say that the husband must have taken the ingots in trade many years back and did not wish to declare them as income while he was alive. He wished instead to leave them for his wife." All's well that ends well. However, this is the exception to financial infidelity and not the rule.

"How do you handle controlling men who wish to control their family finances? "During meetings in which a husband and wife are present a husband tends to ask questions more to impress his wife than to learn. When the wife then asks a question, he dismisses it, citing her financial ignorance." Jay was careful to point out that he is not accepting of a spouse who desires to single-handedly run the financial portfolio but in the cases in which this happens he is careful to determine that the wives (in most cases the spouse is a woman) are neither eager nor interested in getting involved. This, Jay said, is their personal business but does not make sound financial sense.

I couldn't agree more. As a business woman in the practice of therapy, I all too often hear women talk about their disinterest in knowing about or getting involved in their marital or business finances. This is a recipe for disaster! Information is knowledge and knowledge is power. Monitoring the health of one's bank accounts is no less important than monitoring the health of one's emotional and sexual relationship.

CURRENCY REVISITED

Treasure hunt aside, as the aforementioned statistics show, most people see this sort of financial secret keeping as a form of betrayal – and they would be correct. Hillary, whose husband Andrew had "stolen" $100,000, certainly felt this way. In their situation money was a stand in for control. Andrew's anxiety and behavior was based on his need for power and control in his life, not based on reality. If Andrew were to become willing to shift his thinking from fear and control to love and relational sharing, he would start to see his money for what it is and be open to love and support from Hillary. If love and compassion became more important than power and control, Hillary and Andrew might not have relationship problems.

It is important to note the difference between actual money concerns and power struggles over money. A couple can work together towards a shared goal and still not have enough financial resources to go around. When this happens there may not be power struggles so much as actual money concerns. And while it is unfortunate it is also expected.

We'll revisit Hillary and Andrew in Chapter Twelve, "The Experience of Disconnection," but first let's continue our examination of sex, money, and power with the concept of "financial porn."

~~~

QUESTIONS FOR YOURSELF:

- What do I know about my own financial situation?

- Do I choose to be an active participant in financial planning?

- Am I aware of where monies are allocated?

- Do I have any resentment about how money is spent?

- Do I believe that I contribute to my relationship in equal terms? If not, Why?

- What am I willing to do different to become more educated and less vulnerable?

QUESTIONS ABOUT YOUR PARTNER:

- Does my partner include me in financial decision making?

- Is my partner willing to communicate about our finances? If so,

- Is my partner respectful when discussing money or finances?

- Is my partner revealing about where s/he invests or spends money?

- Does my partner contribute less/more than I do?

- Is my partner resentful about that?

CHAPTER 9:

FINANCIAL PORN

On financially transmitted diseases: "Derivatives are like sex. It's not who we're sleeping with, it's who they're sleeping with that's the problem."

— *Warren Buffett*

In an age of round-the-clock news dispatches akin to *heard it before it even happened*, those who are seemingly permanently affixed to their electronic BFF can easily forget what life was like before the Internet, mobile devices, and social media. It's also a wonder that real-world intimacy has a fighting chance against the ever-changing intensity of online experiences. Undeniably, advances in technology have brought tremendous advantages to those who wish to connect when they are geographically or physically separated. Authors Rob Weiss and Jennifer Schneider succeeded in exploring the impact of technology in their book, *Closer Together, Further Apart: The Effect of the Internet and Technology on Parenting, Work and Relationships.* But what happens when people are more focused on working or following their investments than their relationships?

I CAN'T HEAR YOU

This shift toward a constant stream of online information (especially financial information) and away from interpersonal intimacy poses a significant risk to many real-world couples. In fact, I witness this all the time in my therapy sessions with couples. "'You never listen,' has become an epidemic complaint in a world that is exchanging convenience for contact, speed for meaning. As is the case with music, the richness of life doesn't lie in the loudness and the beat, but in the timbres and the variations that you can discern if you simply pay attention."[1] So too is this true in therapy. At the beginning of a session I frequently find myself asking clients to silence their phone (or phones) while we talk. If a one or two-hour therapy session cannot occur without interruption, what's to become of a couple's day-to-day relationship?

"Where was that photo taken?" Rob asked about a nondescript snapshot on my wall.

Rob was a 37-year-old banker who was calmly scanning my office for distraction while his wife Chelsea sat quietly beside him. He was dressed in a striking Dolce & Gabbana Martini suit complete with black Italian leather apron wing Prada shoes – nothing to scoff at. He was the epitome of influence and finesse. However, Rob wasn't trying to make a fashion statement so much as he was striving for a bid at power in this initial session. He didn't need to say, "Back off." His power attire would do this for him. Chelsea sat close beside Rob. However, she would not look at him or even turn in his direction. This was rather telling. The degree to which a client establishes his or her own identity in the session often reflects how a couple operates in their private world. Chelsea seemed far less interested than Rob in establishing any kind of power. In fact, she didn't appear willing to even challenge it in their dynamic.

I answered Rob's question. "In Nepal, as were the others. Have you been there?"

"No, but I will. I'm retiring after I collect my bonus later this year. I'll be doing a lot of traveling. Well, *we'll* be doing a lot of traveling."

"Retire," I asked?

"Yes! Chelsea and I want to take off and get away. Isn't that right?" he told her.

I wondered if Chelsea knew of their plans before now. "Well," I said, "before you both do that maybe you can tell me why you're..." My words were interrupted by Rob's pulsing phone. I hadn't yet asked them to silence their phones, but Chelsea was quick to remind Rob – a request which appeared to be a more a plea than a demand.

Chelsea continued, "I'm concerned about Rob's recovery from sex addiction. You've been looking at porn which I don't understand because you're in recovery for sex addiction for five years now, correct?" Rob sat quiet. "And...," she proceeded with caution as if not to cross a delicate line she was about to breach. "I feel like I have to compete with your phone and your business. I can't remember the last time we had an uninterrupted conversation."

Rob spent a good part of his response reasoning to discredit his wife's concerns, starting with the following: until he retired his business had to come first; he understood money better than she did so she should just let him handle it; his porn use wasn't an issue because he'd only slipped with it "a couple of times" (an accusation of Rob that Chelsea herself wasn't certain was a valid one), and his phones only rang when people really needed to talk to him. Rob finished off his monologue, "If you want to retire early *and be financially comfortable* then I need to keep a constant eye on my business." Almost everything Rob said or did during our session ensured continued distance and disconnect between him and Chelsea. I was particularly concerned about the extent to which Chelsea allowed her reality to be discounted and invalidated.

There is a fine line between passion and obsession, no doubt, and perhaps some of what Rob argued held water. After all, growing and developing a business venture or ventures takes a level of unparalleled dedication. But when a partner registers enough discontent and frustration that she schedules a therapy session to discuss the adverse effects, it is clear that the relationship needs help. For Rob and Chelsea, it remained to be seen where the line would be drawn between legitimate business and disruption from intimacy.

FINANCIAL PORN

Nowhere is this endless informational flow more prized than in the global financial arenas, where information and timing is everything. The timing of an IPO (initial public offering), knowing when to bring a deal to market, or being first to the Bid or the Ask drives financial success.[2] And, thanks to digital devices, the corner office has given way to the corner cushion on the living room couch or the local coffee shop. Keeping up with the latest news, for some, begins to take on an obsessional quality. As is the case with any obsessive behavior or behaviors (sex, work, phone use, and financial issues in Rob's case) the preoccupation inevitably and negatively affects other parts of a person's life. For many, especially those deeply involved in the financial arena, the endless torrent of financial reporting can be escapist and mind-numbing, much like porn, used as a way to dissociate from day-to-day life. In such cases, partners and spouses are often left wondering how and even if they fit into the distracted partner's world.

"When asked for a definition of pornography, Supreme Court Justice Potter Stewart said that although he couldn't formally define it, 'I know it when I see it.' That seems to apply to what Rich Karlgaard (publisher of Forbes Magazine) has evocatively labeled 'financial porn.' Distributed via the Internet for people to read in the dark confines of their own home, financial porn bombards us with lurid images of societal breakdown, catches our eyes with wildly gyrating curves and people losing their shirts by the millions and finally hits us with the (give us your) money shot: a request for your credit card number and a promise that your purchase will provide you with a happy ending."[3]

Financial Porn is a savvy catchphrase for the ever-expanding filler in media and financial coverage. The phrase refers to the "short-term focus by the media on a financial topic that can create excitement but does little to help investors make smart, long-term financial decisions, and in many cases clouds investors' decision-making ability."[4] In this way financial porn is much like sexual porn, which creates temporary excitement but does little to help men and women achieve long-term intimacy. Is it any wonder Rob, in the example above, is hooked on both?

IN THE HEADLINES

If financial porn includes the hyped front page proclamations extolling funds' large fortunes resulting from minimal investments and never-before-seen sector trends and mutual funds of tomorrow, then it's a prime example of what the advertising guys and gals have known all along: sell the sizzle, not the steak. For the uninitiated, knowing what to ignore and what to pay attention to (much less having the self-control to do so) amidst the blitzkrieg of newsworthy and not-so-newsworthy financial news can be easily forgotten in the haze of a mind-numbing trance. Amidst this deluge of distraction, an intimate relationship is most likely relegated to the proverbial back seat. This happens with any form or combination of addictions and certainly when that addiction is to sex, pornography and compulsive masturbation.

My years in finance and as a therapist have taught me many things. Of particular note, I've learned that money and sex make for addictive bedfellows, and they also make for great headlines, titillating scandals, and auctioned movie rights. To most of us, the name of Jordon Belfort is meaningless. Back in the 1990s, when Belfort scammed his brokerage clients out of $100 million, it was marginally newsworthy. That's because the years of financial shell games, unbridled greed, junk bonds, designer drugs, and never-ending sex had yet to reach their blinding zenith. Nevertheless, Mr. Belfort's story is being told in a movie directed by Martin Scorsese, with Leonardo Dicaprio playing Belfort. But why Belfort? And what about Howie Hubler, who scammed his clients at Morgan Stanley out of almost $9 billion in 2007 (Yes, again that's "billion" with a "b.")? Cinematically speaking, Belfort's story is far more interesting because of his notorious drug addiction and sexual escapades.

Cocaine and prostitutes make for great screen fodder. Unfortunately, they also make for real-life disasters.

A PENNY FOR YOUR THOUGHTS?

In a matter of speaking, if there was ever a time to be alive, now is it! The therapist in me says this from the perspective of evolving research into the undiscovered synapses and crevices of the brain and the current advances in understanding the neurobiology of human behavior. The financial trader in me says this from the perspective of advances in economic science, commodity pricing, and business cycles. Back when I was actively trading commodity options I often wondered (and similar thoughts still cross my mind) what traders were thinking as they went about their business.

Beyond the cacophony of noise and undulating intensity on the commodity trading floor, I wondered what lurked deeper within their brain mass. Were they driven by the primal emotions of the market, or was there more to it? After all, if the conversation on the floor wasn't about money, it tended to be about sex. Conversation in the sugar pit between the forty or so male traders and myself seldom strayed from either. But what does sex, you may ask, have to do with sugar options and the likes of money? Well, as far as my male trading counterparts were concerned, and as far as what science now has to disclose – a lot!

If the tools of a financier's trade include investment derivatives, models of risk and uncertainty, and financial instruments, then the tools for many neuropsychologists and researchers now include fMRI and PET scans. Gone are the days of hypotheticals and theories. Brain scans today allow us to observe real-time activation of the pleasure and reward centers in our brains. And when scientists monitor activity in those brain centers while subjects watch porn, they can see what's happening in the brain. The same is true for scientists monitoring brain activity of traders in action. And the brain activity looks shockingly similar! In other words, the brain reacts to sexual stimulation in much the same way it reacts to financial stimulation. Many authors who have written on the subject of pornography addiction have emphasized the rise in compulsivity and addiction due to the internet's relative ease of access, affordability, and anonymity – that Triple A engine effect as it is known.[5] This feedback loop of pleasure is no less powerful when money is factored into the equation.

FINANCIAL AND SEXUAL SUPERCONDUCTORS

When the likes of sexual and financial pornography collide, they sometimes fuse into a superconductor of pleasure and escape. How does this happen and what are the components of brain and behavior that drive this engine? What affects our decision-making process under an onslaught of continual doses of sexual and financial stimuli? A new and growing field called neuroeconomics is attempting to bring the science of brain biology together with psychology and economics to explore exactly why and how we make our decisions.

Let's revisit my male counterparts in the sugar pit. A recent study has helped determine what exactly is going on in the minds of guys like this when they take risky monetary gambles. They're thinking about sex. A group of researchers at Stanford University conducted a study that involved 15 heterosexual young men. What they found was that when these young men were shown erotic pictures they were more likely to make a larger financial gamble than if they were shown an image of something scary or neutral. The brain's reward area lit up at about the same time as risky decision making."[6] In a matter of speaking, the increased activation in the reward area induced a feedback loop leading to higher risk taking. Higher sexual intensity led to higher brain activation which led to higher risk taking which led to more desire for sexual intensity: a self-perpetuating cycle of sexual and financial excess.

This is what I was seeing with Rob, who we met earlier in this chapter. It was clear that he was unwilling to relinquish his attachment to his mobile devices in spite of the fact that it both angered and concerned his wife. The negative consequences of his behavior as he continued to focus on the torrent of financial information (and apparently to pornography as well) was, of course, just the tip of the iceberg for this couple.

Weiss and Schneider write in *Closer Together, Further Apart*:

> *"Although it is easier than ever today to locate and connect with others, many people fail to do so, possibly in part because our electronic means of communication (both sent and received) seem to encourage a greater focus on self than in the past. In other words, digital communication by its very solo nature encourages users to engage in a more frequent and greater display of narcissistic or self-focused traits."*[7]

The fact remained that if Rob was in recovery for sex addiction, yet accessing pornography, then he was not in recovery at all. The very essence of being in recovery means abstaining from substances or behaviors associated with the addiction. Therefore, it was clear that Rob was in denial about his relapse; regardless of how long it had been.

But most importantly and as we've previously explored, addiction is a self-centered state of being. It looks, sounds, and quacks like narcissism. Consider the following excerpt by clinical psychologist and author, Tian Dayton:

> *"The narcissist tends to view other people, not necessarily as individuals in their own right, but as extensions of himself. A narcissist often prefers to have people around him who behave in such a way as to meet and gratify his own needs or enhance his own vision of himself. How does this mirror addiction? Addiction creates a kind of narcissism. It is constantly preoccupying; it takes a person over body, mind and soul. For those who live with an addict, love them and depend on*

them to be at the other end of a relationship, life can be discouraging. It's a lot like living with a narcissist because no matter what you do or how hard you try, you will always come second; second to the addict's pressing needs, second to their constant preoccupations, second to the disease."[8]

Much of my work that day focused on the nature of Rob and Chelsea's struggles and how I could help them. I learned that Chelsea's previous two marriages ended in divorce, so she was not prepared to relinquish this one so quickly. I also learned that she chose to marry men who had a domineering personality and who relegated her to the back seat. As I read between the lines, money and all that it buys took its place of importance in the front seat even if hers was in the back. Rob was not inclined to share much of his personal past and by all accounts never intended to. His presence might have been mandatory; his participation was optional and so it was that I never saw them again.

From that one session I cannot say whether they ever made successful inroads to emotional reconnection or resolution. What I can say is that if they were to connect and build any semblance of true intimacy, Rob had to first confront his obsessions, preoccupations, or addictions. And Chelsea would need to identify her boundaries in the relationship and her pattern of permitting herself to be invalidated and dismissed in their marriage. As Tian wrote, "The narcissist also tends to be absorbed in themselves and in meeting their next need and rather unaware and even uncaring of the needs of those around them." Same with the addict: the needs of those around them have to come second to their meeting their own, often overpowering desire for their next "fix" whether it be drink, drug, food or sexual encounter. Both the narcissist and the addict are first and foremost self-absorbed. In the next chapter we'll explore the eros of money and the preoccupation of work.

~~~

QUESTIONS FOR YOURSELF:

Do You:
- Engage in online behavior to a greater extent or over a longer period than intended?

- Spend time spent in activities necessary for the behavior, engaging in the behavior or recovering from its effects?

- Experience preoccupation with financial accomplishments or information seeking?

- Engage in the behavior when expected to fulfill occupational, academic, domestic, or social obligations?

- Give up or limit important social, occupational, or recreational activities because of the behavior?

- Continue the behavior despite a persistent or recurrent social, financial, psychological, or physical problem?

- Feel restless or irritable if unable to engage in the desired behavior?

- Feel invisible in the relationship?

- Allow yourself to remain silent or invisible?

QUESTIONS ABOUT YOUR PARTNER:

Does Your Partner:
- Frequently engage in online behavior to a greater extent or over a longer period than intended?

- Spend time engaging in online behavior or recovering from its effects?

- Experience preoccupation with financial endeavors or information?

- Engage in the behavior when expected to fulfill occupational, academic, domestic, or social obligations?

- Give up or limit important social, occupational, or recreational activities because of the behavior?

- Continue the behavior despite a persistent or recurrent social, financial, psychological, or physical problem?

- Feel restless or irritable if unable to engage in the desired behavior?

- Feel invisible in the relationship?

- Emotionally, physically or sexually bully or manipulate you?

CHAPTER 10

MONEY AS AN APHRODISIAC

America does not know the difference between money and sex. It treats sex like money because it treats sex as a medium of exchange, and it treats money like sex because it expects its money to get pregnant and reproduce.

— Peter Kreeft, How to Win the Culture War: A Christian Battle Plan for a Society in Crisis

Like many, I can only observe financial and economic ramifications of political events in hindsight. But, unlike many, I have had on a few very interesting occasions a front-row seat that allowed me to witness history unfolding in real time. One such day was January 9, 1991. I was still trading options in the sugar pit and my husband at the time was a trader in the "oil complex." On that day the oil markets were dynamic even more than usual as the United States and its allied forces were on the brink of war with Iraq.

THE HOUSE THAT SADDAM BUILT

In the final hours leading to either a hopeful diplomatic resolution or the outbreak of war, Secretary of State James Baker sat across the table from Tariq Aziz, who was Saddam Hussein's Iraqi Foreign Minister and closest adviser. The Geneva Peace Conference was a last-ditch effort to avoid a war precipitated by Iraq's refusal to remove its occupying forces from Kuwait. For obvious reasons the United States and its allies had been pressing for an immediate withdrawal; for equally obvious reasons Iraq was refusing to comply. On that January day, Baker and Aziz talked. Various heads of state sat poised in the wings, anticipating international diplomacy or chaos and the world's financial and economic markets also sat in wait – much was hanging in the balance.

As most readers are aware, the Geneva Peace Conference did not end well. The meeting resulted in no significant progress toward a resolution to the Iraqi occupation of Kuwait. Immediately following the breakdown to any compromise, the "oil complex," where my husband worked, launched itself into a frenzy. The global markets were so chaotic that Baker later commented:

> *"Someone told me afterwards that the first word I used was "regrettably," and when I said "regrettably" there was a tremendous amount of market activity in the various markets around the world, world markets and stock markets and so forth. And everybody concluded just from that one word that, that things were not going to work out politically, that we probably would end up at war in the Persian Gulf."*[1]

Baker's statement is entirely accurate. As swift as a lightning strike, adrenaline, fear, and exhilaration swept through the markets. On the trading floor at the World Trade Center oil traders felt the panic. When the news broke they frantically aborted whatever else they were doing and sprinted from all reaches of the building back to the crude oil pit.

It wasn't just in the crude oil pit that the market reacted. As Baker's statement revealed, fear was contagious. In one split second all global stock markets, oil markets and corporate financial deals shifted violently from the political fallout in Geneva. In the blink of an eye financial fortunes were both lost and amassed depending on which way your trading position was caught.

MORE-GASMS

The only thing that traders like more than volatile markets are *lucrative* volatile markets. For a trader, what good is intensity without the payoff? And there's more to the payoff than mere money. A survey conducted in 2007 found that 70% of multimillionaires said being wealthy offered them "better sex." [2] And there may be a good reason for that. If money relieves stressors that plague most of us, the very rich – or at least those richer than the majority of us—can relax into the moment and fully enjoy their "happy endings." Having a financial cushion to fall back on goes a long way to alleviating financial tensions that come with life's vicissitudes, especially if your cushion happens to be located in exotic and faraway places. In fact, a majority of the multimillionaires surveyed said that in addition to better sex, their wealth gave them access to "more adventurous and exotic" sex. Another study, this one conducted at Newcastle University in 2009, revealed that women experience a higher frequency of orgasms as their partner's income increased.

In addition to better sex, more exotic sex, and increased potential for orgasm, research has found that increases in money, power, and wealth are linked to a higher likelihood of infidelity. A study published in the *Journal of Marital and Family Therapy* indicated that men who earn more money have a higher likelihood of cheating than those who earn less. MSNBC also conducted a survey on the subject of love and fidelity. According to the survey, 32% of men making more than $300,000 a year reported cheating compared to 21% of men who made less than $35,000 a year. Clearly, high-risk financial pursuits such as mergers and acquisitions, high-stakes gambling, stocks and bonds, as well as commodity trading also feed off of high-risk sex. In other words, risk, power, and reward are arousing, and money is an aphrodisiac.

ALL WORK AND NO PLAY...

It's no secret that capitalism is rarely motivated by altruism. The only self-sacrifice made in a capitalist world is in the love and relationship department, and even then the motivations are somewhat murky, as for many individuals money equals love. When that is the case, emotional availability takes a back seat to the pursuit of money, power, and control. The people on this insatiable quest for all things green and dandy (and therefore sexy) were nearly always deprived of intimacy and affection in childhood. Such people learn early on to seek substitutes as a way of meeting or masking their needs. Money, sex, and adulation become a stand-in for healthy emotional connection. Adam, who we met in Part One, came to resent his family's money because they gave material goods instead of actively showing and sharing affection. As a result Adam struggled with loneliness throughout his life.

Money obsession, workaholism, high adrenaline jobs and sex are aphrodisiacs to many and addictive to some. One woman who knows this all too well is Bonnie DenDooven. At first glance what one notices about Bonnie is her peaceful demeanour, sparkly eyes, radiant smile and dimpled cheeks. But sweetness aside, Bonnie is an unflappable woman whose previous career in business helped mold her into the skillful therapist she is today and an unlikely appraiser of compulsive patterns around money and work. As a therapist, however, all of those traits work squarely in her favor especially when she is delivering exactly what a client should hear but would choose not to know; all with such disarming candor. Her financial experience and passion for helping others fed her fascination in the creation of the Money and Work Adaptive Styles Index© (MAWASI), with Dr. Patrick Carnes, an assessment tool that evaluates difficulty with money and work issues.[5]

Dr. Carnes may have brought the issue of sex addiction out of the shadows with his groundbreaking publication of the same name.

However, it was Bonnie's passion that brought the issue of compulsive financial and work behaviours out of their shadow and into the light. On this playing field, money IS the object of affection. As one study revealed, women may say they are looking for tight abs or a sense of humor in their man, but he had better have a healthy bank balance to go with it. "That makes it hard to compete for attention when all you have is a cleft chin, wavy hair, and six-pack abs."[6]

...MAKES JACK A DULL BOY

Another controversial study, published in January 2011 by London School of Economics' Professor Dr. Catherine Hakim, found that more women were said to prefer to marry a man earning more than they do. In that poll, "64 per cent said they aspire to find a husband bringing home more money. None wanted to marry a man who earned less."(Hakim[7]) According to Dr. Hakim more women were choosing to 'marry up' by picking wealthy men for their spouse than in the 1940s.

So, why is it that women find money so attractive? Many researchers believe that on an evolutionary level, a powerful mate affords a woman protection and a guarantee of food and shelter. "If," says Dr. Buss, an evolutionary psychologist from The University of Texas at Austin, "Money and wealth signifies security, then it can be exchanged for things important to a woman's wellbeing, such as food or protection – or shoes." His research with Dr. Cindy M. Meston, a sexual psychophysiologist, is published in their coauthored book, *Why Women Have Sex*. From an evolutionary perspective money equates to power or at the least being resourceful and powerful equates to intelligence. Intelligence, it seems, is linked to resource acquisition, and since it's heritable, it signals 'good genes' for a woman's progeny and survival of the fittest.

The downfall of former CIA chief General David Petraeus – forced to resign after revelations of an affair with his biographer Paula Broadwell – was splashed across the headlines in late 2012. It seemed that all that hard work for General Petraeus did pay off but not for the assumed reasons.

Petraeus may have been the highest ranking military leader in all the land, but it most likely wasn't his good looks that got him there and most likely not what led Paula Broadwell to burn the midnight oil.

The veritable fact is that power and money may be two of the most potent sexual stimulants known, perhaps even more effective than chocolate and Viagra combined. Since the first caveman learned to make fire men and women have been playing power games. Fast-forward several thousand years and power, influence and wealth are still making a difference. Although money and power can provide financial stability, it may lag far behind in the emotional security department. While many of those surveyed report dollar-and-cents arousal, like most things new and novel, aphrodisiacs will eventually dissolve and go the way of short-term attractors. Therefore, healthy longer-term relationships need more than just money and as we've seen from so many examples in this book – plenty of money does not make for love or affection.

~~~

QUESTIONS FOR YOURSELF:

- What role does money play in my life?

- What meaning does money have for me?

- Does it represent acceptance, status, power, or even love?

- Do I accept money or material items instead of love and affection?

- When and where did I learn to settle for money in lieu of love and affection?

- In lieu of love, what substitutes do I use (sex, money, food, gambling, spending)?

- In my life, where have I learned to accept less?

QUESTIONS ABOUT YOUR PARTNER:

- What role does money play in your partner's life?

- What meaning does money have for your partner or spouse?

- Does it represent acceptance, status, power, or even love?

- Does your partner accept money or material items instead of love and affection?

- When and where did your partner learn to settle for money in lieu of love and affection?

- In lieu of love, what substitutes does your partner use (sex, money, food, gambling, spending)?

- In my life, where did your partner learn to accept less?

CHAPTER 11

MONETIZED RAGE

The kind of personality that rises to the top of shark-infested professions like politics and finance tends to be ruthless, fearless, charming, and often (more often than not I would say), somewhat lacking in the conscience department.

— *Kevin Dutton, Ph.D.*

In Chapter Six, "Eroticized Rage," we explored patterns of sexual arousal that are fed by elements of revenge, entitlement, and resentment. This arousal pattern is based on shame turned into anger, and it often involves covert or overt levels of abuse and possibly even violence. Drawing from the same underlying manifestations is another arousal pattern, one based on monetary and financial exploitation which I refer to as "monetized rage."

A year ago, Dr. Carnes invited me to come and train the staff of a noted treatment center. I began to lecture on the concept of eroticized rage and in that moment the thought dawned on us both that sexualized anger (eroticized rage) and monetized anger are driven by the same underlying issues. Since that time we have come to refer to monetized anger as "monetized rage." Monetized rage (MR) behaviors have a close relationship with eroticized rage (ER) behaviors, as both sets of actions involve control and exploitation through rage, contempt, disdain, and perverse entitlement. However, whereas ER speaks to the fusion of anger and eroticism, MR speaks to the synthesis of anger and money. Of significance is that these two forms of anger are not mutually exclusive.

When money and sex are fused in the service of exploitation, the two create an even more destructive form of rage of a type often exhibited in narcissistic and potentially psychopathic populations. Kevin Dutton, a psychologist and Research Fellow of the Faraday Institute at St. Edmunds College, UK, believes that psychopathy often flourishes in professions like politics and finance, where the ruthless, fearless, and (dare I say) charming qualities typically lead to success, power, and prestige. As Dr. Dutton writes:

> *"It has traditionally been thought that psychopaths are all bad. Psychopaths are very good at persuasion due to a trait known as cold empathy. Our personalities are a mixture of elements with some turned up, and others turned down. There are jobs where high scores on the psychopathic spectrum can be advantageous, such as some areas of intricate, high risk surgery. People think that psychopaths do not have empathy, and that is true in the sense that they don't have hot empathy, they aren't able to really feel what you and I might be feeling. But what they are very good at is gauging cognitively and dispassionately what we might be feeling. They're very good actors. And of course if you don't have those attendant hot buttons that go with sensing what state another person might be in, you can very easily push those buttons yourself without getting caught up in the heat of the moment."[1]*

In other words, scoring high on the psychopathy scale is not a bad thing. In fact, in some professions it's a tremendous asset. Military leaders, surgeons, and professional athletes often need to be able to act with cold-blooded precision. If they cave into emotional pressure, especially the pressure of someone else's emotions, they're not likely going to be any good at their job. Unfortunately, these individuals are also ripe for both eroticized and monetized rage, either of which can create significant problems in their personal lives.

Certainly, MR, like ER, is opportunistic and frequently rooted in deep angry feelings that justify exploitation for personal gain, behaviors that are synonymous with narcissism. Studies have suggested that narcissists crave authority and power, assume self-entitlement, hold biased views of the self, exploit social relationships, and possess high self-esteem.[2]

Similar to Ron and Chelsea's story in Chapter Nine, "Financial Porn," addicts of all types who are in the throes of their addiction often exploit with sex and money, regardless of their level of wealth or income, and they don't have to be psychopaths or even innately narcissistic to do so. Addicts may go into debt in order to sustain their level of addiction, a level of lavish spending or impression management. They certainly do so as it pertains to sexual access. That said most addicts and most people who display ER/MR also display the main characteristics of narcissistic personality disorder (NPD). Common traits of a narcissistic personality include:

- Taking advantage of others to achieve their goals.

- A preoccupation or obsession with fantasies that focus on exaggerated success, power, intelligence, approval and acceptance.

- Belief in one's uniqueness.

- A belief that they can only be understood by other special people.

• Inability to recognize or identify with the feelings, needs, and perspectives of others – lack of empathy or compassion.

 • Envy of others or a belief that others are envious of him or her.

 • Hypersensitivity to criticism or defeat.

 • Arrogant behavior and/or attitude

PAY TO PLAY

A clinical subscale of the Sexual Dependency Inventory-Revised (SDI-R) – an assessment often used in the diagnosis and treatment of sex addicts – identifies financial preoccupation as an overlay to sexual activities. At a minimum money becomes sexually enhanced and little more than a business transaction or an avenue for exploitation. In this case, money is often a part of the experience (exchanging money, dinner, gifts, and similar currency for sex). Over time, the arousal can become more about the payment than about the sex and money and sex becomes entwined with self-righteous entitlement. Consider the following:

• Arranging financial support for someone in order to ensure control and power.

 • Giving or receiving money in order to control or manipulate another person.

• Providing employment to a financially vulnerable individual in order to gain personal or professional control or access.

• Using money to threaten an individual into being compliant sexually or otherwise.

• Sending or giving gifts to people in an attempt to elicit sexual favors.

The previous statements describe those who use power, money and position as exploitive tools for manipulation and control may not outwardly display a rageful presentation. Most people who hear the word "rage" imagine violent anger, fury, screaming or physical abuse but rage comes in many forms including covert. For some people in relationship, being angry reminds them of a violent, angry and destructive person: a behavior to be avoided at all costs; however, eroticized or monetized rage is often conveyed in silent or passive aggressive ways and therefore goes unnoticed. Something may feel amiss, but "I don't see anything wrong, so I don't think there is a problem," is a common statement I hear from clients. The behavior parades in full view without outward signs of detection or alarm.

IT'S ALL THE RAGE

The tension between thought and feeling is palpable in many therapists' offices, mine included, so today was no different than usual. "Anger is an emotion. Rage is more of a behavior." I said.

"Yes, I know," my client Wayne responded. "But to say that rage is not actually an emotion I find hard to believe!"

"Consider it to be anger on steroids," I said.

I often explain to my clients that rage is a stress response activated within the nervous system. This flight-or-fight response occurs when we experience what we perceive to be a real or imagined threat. However, what you perceive as a threat may have one meaning for you and another completely different for someone else. An example may be a derisive statement made about you that slices deep into your buried, inner shame core – a dagger that pierces the delicate veil protecting your easily humiliated ego. Or, it's an actual threat to your or a loved one's existence. Hormones such as oxytocin, vasopressin, and other peptide hormones are released from within the brain, the hypothalamus to be exact, which drive this response.

Wayne started therapy to resolve an internal disequilibrium. As a result of his individual and group therapy, he'd learned to understand that his shame, grievances, and deep insecurity left a gaping void that he filled with sex, money, and anything else that would deliver relief from feeling less than. Like many of the men I treat, this inner void drove Wayne's outward behavior as he sought to compensate with ever increasing levels of thrill, accomplishment, approval, and power: all of the things that eluded him in childhood.

The wealth and prestige that Wayne reaped from his business ventures were both his deliverance and his ruination. He grew up in New York as the son of a successful and vindictive businessman. He often heard his father say "Let them hate me, so long as they also fear me," when describing his business conquests. This quote, initially attributed to Caligula during his reign of terror and gluttony, made for a frightening childhood. "Money equalled love, and money equalled approval. In order to be loved by my dad I had to win his approval. That meant that I had to succeed in school because succeeding in school meant I would also succeed in business when I grew up," Wayne told me during one of our sessions.

Needless to say, Wayne's wealthy family had entrée to financial and social largesse.

"Exotic and erotic," he said.

"As I got older I learned that women could always be bought; it was just a matter of price. My father taught me this through example when he brought me into the business. I quickly became his most trusted business partner. For both of us, money and sex were a sport."

Wayne looked both prideful and empty as he told me about this aspect of his past life.

"Eventually I began to hate what it all meant. I became someone I didn't want to be, just to win my father's approval. Finally, I decided that I just couldn't do it anymore and left the business. With my father, you're either with him or against him. When I decided that I could no longer continue the lifestyle of his shady business deals, women, and drinking he turned his wrath on me. There was no finding my own self as far as he was concerned. In his world, choosing me meant betraying him, and he took my decision as a personal insult."

Wayne then described years of acrimony and family lawsuits, all the result of vain attempts to gain his father's approval.

WE LEARN WHAT WE LIVE

Like many who are the sons and daughters of strong-willed and potentially influential businessmen, Wayne learned what he lived: that money stood for control and power. As Terrence Real described in his book, *I Don't Want To Talk About It: Overcoming The Secret Legacy of Male Depression*: "Narcissus in love with his image is like a man in love with his bank account, his good looks or his power. Narcissus is an emblem for all men enthralled with just about anything other than their own deepest selves." In other words, many narcissists' primary relationship is with money. Wayne's was, and it cost him dearly. Both he and his father became financially rich but relationally poor and like a lot of narcissists, Wayne learned to compensate for his "lesser self" by earning a lot of money and using it to control others. As part of this, his life became consumed with mistresses and escorts. The more financially vulnerable the women were the more powerful and in control he felt.

Wayne's downfall came in a perverse twist of reality. During his reign of money, rage and entitlement, he became obsessed with the need for a particular mistress's undivided attention. His grip on reality slipped badly and he was consumed by jealousy. He began to stalk and threaten her. Before long the exploiter became the exploited; the perpetrator the prey. In a rageful reprisal, the mistress called Wayne's wife and his business partners to reveal his reckless behavior. As is always the case, what goes up must come down and so it was the Icarus Complex all over again. Wayne's magical thinking led to an ascent quickly followed by ruin and dissolution. Both the internalized and projected fantasy had fallen. Icarus was dead.

WINGS OF WAX

Other men have experienced similar days of reckoning:

- I've always dated women who were needier than me. This way I could control them and feel superior. I dated women not because I liked being with them but because they looked good with me. I know that there's something wrong with my thinking, but it's taking time to change. I've stopped dating altogether so I can begin to understand me. I want to date women because I like being with them, not because I can seduce them. I want to like them.

- My wife ran up huge credit card debt. I never said no to any purchases. After all, I was being dishonest by having affairs and spending crazy sums of money on prostitutes. I saw this as my penance for what I was doing. Eventually I declared bankruptcy, not because I wasn't earning a really good living, but because I was letting my wife spend crazy amounts of money as a result of what I was doing.

- Growing up I always felt so weak. So when I became an adult I made the decision to never let go of the control. By controlling money and everyone around me, I always felt stronger and more powerful. But that drove people away, including my children. No matter how powerful I became I still felt pathetic.

Because these men as children never learned how to relate or to tolerate emotions they never learned how to tolerate dis-ease both within themselves and in relationships. Being vulnerable only offered an opportunity to those around them to be ridiculed or abused. As such, intensity and fear replaced intimacy and connection, and seduction became a substitute and controlling stand-in for connection. Below is a list that may help you identify ways in which you either engage in monetized rage or experience it in your relationships:

THE ADDICT'S MONETIZED RAGE CHECK LIST

 • I control access to household money: you don't know how much or where it is.

 • I control all financial decisions and signatures on accounts.

 • My partner has to account for all his/her expenditures. I get angry when there are unexplained expenses.

- I protect my partner from knowing the finances or seeking employment.

- I prefer that my partner concentrate on my needs and the marriage.

- I feel high or get a rush when I think about money.

- I'm not ever happy with my lifestyle, even though people tell me they are envious of me.

- I am never sure if people like me or my money.

- I believe that I am entitled to special privileges because of who I am.

- I define success based on my income and material wealth

- I am obsessed with how much my partner spends

- I believe no one would like me unless I had money and paid for their expenses.

- Money gives me a feeling of power and control.

- Despite my income and expenditures, I don't feel better about myself.

- My worth is based on my possessions.

- I demand respect from those that I pay for or support.

- I worry that if I don't pay for others they will leave me.

- I am nothing if I do not control how others view me.

- I have lied to conceal my financial income.

- I have lied about my financial worth so that others will think better of me.

- I value money above all else. I expect others to feel the same.

- Money equals love.

- Love is based on how much money I have.

- I will accrue debt just to keep people financially dependent on me.

THE PARTNER'S MONETIZED RAGE CHECK LIST

- I am afraid of my partner.

- I have to account for all my expenditures. My partner gets angry when I have unexplained expenses.

- I cannot afford to leave my partner. If I did I would be threatened with financial impoverishment.

- I am afraid to ask for more money.

- If I am sexual, I will be loved.

- If I am sexual, I will earn my status as a partner/wife/girlfriend.

- My partner needs increasing intensity in our sex life.

- My partner is not happy unless I escalate the intensity of our sex life.

- I sometimes feel like a hired sex worker, as if I should be paid for what I do in the bedroom.

- I allow people to control me with money.

- I allow people to control me with a certain lifestyle.

- I pay for my lifestyle by being sexual.

- My partner's job is to make the money; my job is to satisfy him sexually.

- I don't value my self-worth.

- I am only as lovable as my possessions.

- I fear retribution if I don't look or act a certain way for my partner.

- If I don't look good for my partner, he will be disappointed in me.

- I resent my life but I don't see any way out.

- I allow people to rescue me with money.

- I sometimes feel like a high-priced escort.

- My partner does not value my contributions to the partnership.

- I don't value my contributions to the partnership.

PART III:

BACK FROM THE BRINK

Man can no longer live for himself alone. We must realize that all life is valuable and that we are united to all life. From this knowledge comes our spiritual relationship with the universe.

— *Albert Schweitzer*

The men were silent. They sat quietly while Joe shared the events of his life that led to his joining my weekly men's sex addiction group. He was in the process of introducing himself when I thought back to his first visit with me. It was hard to imagine that Joe, (who we read about in Chapter Seven, "Icarus Revisited,") was the same man who sat defiant in my office months earlier, contemptuous and impervious to vulnerability. Back then Joe professed that his only problem was his wife:

"She was the one who should realize there's no way in hell she'll continue to have the lifestyle that she demands if I'm not putting in the hours!"

He was also quite contemptuous of the fact that if she wasn't so reactive and uptight about sex he would tell her. In spite of his arrogance, I extended understanding and equanimity because no matter how acerbic Joe was, I knew that behind his caustic and off-putting manner was a fragile ego. Even as I encouraged him to consider attending an intensive men's workshop for professionals he held steadfast and resolute that he didn't have a problem.

"A workshop? Why would I do that? I don't want to do therapy, let alone a workshop!"

"Because it seems that it is hard for you to *not* work compulsively, drink and view pornography for more than two days at a time. These are all the things that keep you from connecting to your feelings." I continued, "And I think that being in a workshop outside of your comfort zone with other men like yourself will make it easier for you to drop your need for impression management and if for nothing else, just hear what others are going through. It might be very helpful for you; more helpful than say, therapy with me, at least for now."

I hoped that over time Joe would be open to some help but he held fast to his entitlement rather than suffer the malaise of appearing ordinary to the world and to me. When this happens, I let go of any expectations for my client and recognize that I may want more for them than they want for themselves. However, in a matter of a month I received a phone call from Joe.

"I took your advice and I'm going to do a workshop."

"Wow…Joe, I'm…*quite* surprised." (Amazed actually) "What changed your mind?"

"I had an incident here and I think that taking your advice might be a good idea."

It was highly unlikely that Joe arrived at this decision voluntarily. Joe's initial reason for coming to therapy was prompted by an edict from his wife. She had threatened him with the prospect of divorce and, given the alternative, Joe made an appointment – albeit begrudgingly. But although little work was done in that initial session, Joe revealed one significant piece of information about himself: Joe would continue to do what he wanted until he could no longer get away with it. That time, I thought, must be now.

"I got a phone call from a prostitute's boyfriend. I don't know how he did it but he had information about me. He threatened to tell my wife and my colleagues if I didn't pay them money. I think he meant it so I told my wife and then I called the police on that SOB."

For the first time I heard mild concern in Joe's voice, enough so that he told his wife and then retreated for the safe haven of a workshop. In his egotistical fashion, Joe believed that he was going to work on his "fondness for the female form, love of alcohol and over active work ethic." What Joe never believed was that he would experience a searing and painful memory about his abusive childhood.

Joe, the twenty-first century Icarus Man fell to earth in his crisis, crumpled wings and all. My attention came back to the group as Joe continued with his story.

"During my intensive workshop, I had an epiphany of sorts. As a part of the work I was instructed to write a letter to my wife and grown children. My assignment was to describe the ways in which I use alcohol, work and pornography to avoid feelings. The night I sat down to write the letter…"

"He paused."

"I don't know why…but I began to think about my grown sons and my childhood. I don't know…I remembered a time when my dad was beating my sister and I tried to stop him but I couldn't. I felt like such a failure. Anyway, I started crying and I couldn't stop."

Joe certainly was moved by this memory and although it was painful it fostered his humility and eventual motivation for change.

"I realized when I wrote my letter how much time I lost with my kids. I will never get those years back – never. I was so busy running; I still am. And I realized that night how much guilt and pain I have about it that it tore me a part. Go figure! I'm trying to somehow make up for lost time with them by doing everything and anything I can for them now."

Joe emailed his letter from the workshop. When his son's responded they shared their love and acceptance but also their sadness: things that they had never shared before. In the end it wasn't their rejection (as he had feared it would be) that caused him the most grief, but their love and acceptance that prompted him to see what he had missed all those years. Joe was so shaken by this that he finished the intensive and continued with another two weeks in the program before he returned to individual and group therapy with me.

Most of these seven men were, at one time or another, apex predators: alpha males with few to no perceived threats of their own. These men enjoyed their power at the top of their personal food chain, garnering accolades and handsome salaries and bonuses. In some cases they may not have made a lot of money, but controlled loved ones in their life as if they did. But now each of these men was a more humbled shade of their former overconfident selves, as they made their way through treatment for trauma and addiction with twelve-step meetings, sponsors, individual therapy, and men's group. Yet why was it that most of them were only *now* confronting the depths of their narcissistic wounding? And why is that it was happening after months of therapy?

Much like Joe, many remain trapped in their own web of denial. The denial becomes a self-fulfilling feedback loop of false resilience reinforced by the humiliation of neglect and abuse that they received throughout their lives. After the veil of their false self was lifted it had to be deconstructed (discussed in Chapter Four, "Emotional Scarcity, Sexual Surplus") before a new and vulnerable self could take shape and develop. That journey, as we read, is *a delicate balance between insight into one's desire for escape and abstinence from one's addiction.*

For those who seek help, before any insight can take root, active addictions (alcohol, drugs, food, work, gambling) must first be addressed and their false thinking (rationalizations and secrecy) protecting the behaviors must be confronted. In the case of sexual compulsivity or addiction those who sexualize or objectify, for example, must interrupt their own excuses. *If my wife (partner) was more sexual or we had a better sex life I wouldn't need to compulsively masturbate, look at porn, or... (fill in the blank).* Further complicating these rationalizations is the fact that these same men de-sexualize their wives which is the flip side of the sexually obsessive coin.

Joe, I am happy to say, came to see me as a champion of his cause rather than the soul slayer he first perceived me to be. His work in group and individual therapy continued to reinforce the skills he learned for building a new connection with his family. For that matter, group helped all these men tear down their old barriers to intimacy and forge new ways to emotionally interact with those around them.

CHAPTER 12

THE EXPERIENCE OF DISCONNECTION

It is not a lack of love, but a lack of friendship that makes unhappy marriages.

— *Friedrich Nietzsche*

It was a brutal summer day in late August when I reviewed the day's appointments. Despite my twenty years in Arizona, I've only grown less, not more, tolerant of Arizona's summers. I was hoping that today's appointments would be less horrific than the weather. In a therapist's office some days are tougher than others: first-time clients bring their fear and anxiety, spouses struggle with the pain of their partner's extramarital sexual behavior, and couples attempt to find their way with any range of communication skills in tow.

You may remember Hillary and Andrew from Chapter Eight, "Financial Infidelity." Hillary was trying to work on the marriage or, more likely, divorcing Andrew after learning about his financial infidelity. Since then, Andrew left for inpatient treatment, and Hillary and I met several more times. Following her last individual session we agreed to reconvene when Andrew returned. Sometime later Hillary called me.

"Andrew is due home, so I would like to schedule a follow-up appointment for us. I think before I come in that we need a plan of action. Andrew and I had a family session while he was away, but that didn't really address the full extent of where we need to go. It was more about him getting things off his chest than it was a help for me. But to be completely honest with you, Deb, I'm not sure what I want to discuss."

"I understand," I said. "You both have a lot of work to do, and I'm hoping that in this session we can decide on the therapeutic direction to take for the two of you as a couple and individually."

"I've been," and here Hillary paused for a long while, "doing a lot of thinking." "And?"

"Well, maybe it's better if we just continue this conversation in your office when the three of us are together."

"Sure," I said. "See you then."

WHERE WE GO FROM HERE

Their appointment was scheduled for this oppressively hot day in July. I couldn't help wonder if the intensity inside my office would exceed the intensity of the heat outside. My gut told me that Hillary was still thinking very seriously about exiting the marriage, but this belief was predicated more on instinct than anything she'd told me in our last few sessions. I hoped that I was wrong. Finally, the appointment time arrived. I showed Andrew and Hillary into my office, and watched them sit on opposite ends of the couch. They were silent for a few moments, until Andrew broke the silence.

"I know that I've made mistakes, but I'm hoping that you'll continue to fight for us." He then added, "I want us to be friends again." Andrew spent a month away, sorting out the inner storms behind his mask while Hillary struggled to hold their finances and life together. Like many people just out of treatment, Andrew felt he had excavated all that there was to know. Now that I've confronted all of my demons shouldn't everything go back to normal, he thought? Of course, he had barely scratched the surface.

Andrew had grown up with an emotionally unavailable father and a suffocating yet distant, narcissistic mother. This distant yet enmeshing experience made for a lonely childhood. Yet Andrew had grown up unaware of the emotional fissures deep within his developing personality. His covert depression was fueled by an inner self-loathing that over time could not sustain a healthy relationship with himself, let alone with a wife. It was only a matter of time before Andrew and his marriage buckled under the pressure.

Hillary choked back tears and spoke. "We never were friends. You've made me believe that I'm to blame for all of your problems. It's only after I pulled the plug on your crazy-making behavior that you decided to get help. I'm not willing to put myself through another round of this. I appreciate you opening up to talk about your past and I have forgiven you but I now realize that I need more; more than you can ever give me."

Her anger had now dissolved, and in its place was clarity.

"I'm sorry, but I'm done. I'm just done. I want different. I want someone who will champion my cause, someone who will be there for me."

Here there was a long, quiet pause.

"I've taken all the lying, all the abuse that I am going to take. I'm no longer angry with you, Andrew, or at you. I've just had enough and I want out."

The end of a marriage is never easy to witness especially if one of the two partners has called it quits while the other clings to hope. Although I am a therapist and well versed in the skills of relationship building, I am not capable of reviving a marriage that is not wishing to be revived. That was the case here. Andrew had nothing to add. He knew this was it. Hillary and Andrew sat quietly on the couch. As their therapist, I too felt the pain of a marriage that was no longer worth fighting for.

The good news, in my practice, at least, is that Hillary and Andrew's experience is the exception rather than the rule. Most of the couples who come to therapy are grappling with sexually and financially exploitive behaviors that have surfaced after a crisis. But unlike Hillary and Andrew, they nearly always believe that their relationship is worth saving and they nearly always manage to stay together – stronger and happier for the effort they put forth.

Yes, the individuals and couples who seek therapy may do so because they are pulled apart by betrayal or addiction. Regardless of what the addictions are, if they continue to be the elephant in the room then nothing can change. It is true that couples who want to stay together will face a tough challenge that will involve painful, unpleasant work. Nevertheless, most of my clients are willing to walk through the pain. Doing so, and developing the tools for a better life, is the focus of the next two chapters.

CHAPTER 13

SPOKEN AGREEMENTS AND SILENT ARRANGEMENTS

Chains of habit are too light to be felt until they are too heavy to be broken.

— *Warren Buffet*

I am a middle-aged white woman, (past middle-aged if I take the true definition into consideration) a mother, partner, therapist, daughter, and sister. The list of things I would do for my sons, partner, clients, mother, and siblings is long and heartfelt. However, as a result of recovery I am now keenly aware that in order to show up for another person I must first be willing to show up for myself. I must face my life on life's terms. For me to ignore what reality serves up and to fight against it is the epitome of insanity, and it inevitably leads to a lot of torment. Of course, this was a lesson I had to learn the hard way.

In 1994, my husband came home one night and made an announcement: "I can't continue this grinding commute into the city!" He worked as a trader on Wall Street, and we had moved out of Manhattan to the suburbs after we started a family. I'd left the trading floor just prior to the birth of my first child so I understood the toll that commuting exacted. Two hours of driving through heavy traffic to the water ferry, parking, crossing the Hudson, and then walking to the office every morning, two more hours of the reverse routine at night – this on top of a grueling, stressful, ultra-intense workday. So I said to him, "I think you should do whatever makes you happy. I understand what you're going through, and I will support you no matter what you decide." He walked off and began his quest for newer, greener career pastures that did not involve a long commute. His quest ended some months later when he boldly announced, "We're moving to Tucson!"

At that point, I began to rethink my offer of support. Apparently I'd omitted the caveat that my enduring support went only so far as the Tristate area? "Where?" I asked.

In response, he told me we'd just purchased a manufacturing business in Tucson, Arizona.

I could little imagine living anywhere other than New York, the hub of the known universe, let alone in the desert. I may have completed my Master of Business Administration at Thunderbird School of International Management in Phoenix, but that was the last time I thought I would feel the blast furnace of summer. However, I agreed to the move with the understanding that the move was temporary. Our spoken agreement at that moment was that he would run the Tucson-based business for three years while we put a management team in place, and then we would move back to New York. But even then I knew this wasn't likely. Outwardly I said yes, expressing full agreement with the plan. Inwardly, I knew that we would not be returning to New York, or at least anytime soon. My spoken agreement satisfied my husband's desire; the silent arrangement was something I had yet to reckon with.

A SILENT PARTNERSHIP

The ways in which partners and spouses are willing to "show up" or be emotionally present and engaged with each other (and themselves) often points to the heart of relational disputes. I often tell my clients, "There is the information we need but do not ask for, and the information we already have yet choose to ignore." The arrangements that couples script are laden with spoken agreements and silent arrangements, to themselves or to another. And the struggles many couples experience are the direct result of these conscious decisions made or avoided. My experience with my then-husband and our move to Tucson is not unique. I am not the only person to ever verbally agree to something while silently ignoring the implications of that arrangement. I often encounter this dynamic in my practice. Kelly and Shawn, who'd been together for eight years, are one such example. During a particularly tense session of couple's therapy Kelly turned to Shawn and said, "You agreed that you would work at paying down your debt, but I don't see that you are doing that!" Shawn responded with anger.

"What right do you have to accuse me when I work hard every day, just as hard as you do?" Kelly was about to go for his therapeutic jugular when I interrupted her. "Kelly, when you met Shawn what information did you have about his financial situation, and what information did you choose to ignore?" Kelly then admitted that when they met Shawn had just come out of a recent bankruptcy and his financial situation was fragile. Nevertheless, she started dating him anyway. As Kelly described it, "Shawn was reeling from a business deal gone awry, and he was doing the best he could to get back on his feet."

As their relationship progressed, Shawn promised Kelly that, because of his business acumen, his situation was sure to be short-lived and that he could and would bounce back.

Although Shawn's promise of financial recovery never seemed to materialize, the two moved in together early in their relationship. Before long, of course, they started arguing about finances. Every few months they came to resolve their issues in therapy, only to back away from the most obvious of issues between them; Kelly agreed to move in with Shawn based on what she already knew but chose to ignore. The larger issue was just beyond recognition – that Shawn was not nearly as good with making and managing money as he professed to be.

IGNORING OUR NEEDS AND WANTS

Many (perhaps most) relationships operate on two levels of understanding. The first level consists of agreements we make based on information that we know or have. The second level consists of the silent arrangements we make based on the information that we choose to ignore, or, worse still, the agreements we make while intentionally avoiding asking for the pertinent information we so desperately need in order to make a healthy decision.

In Kelly's case, she knew about Shawn's financial situation but chose to ignore the fact that he had recently experienced a bankruptcy and was struggling to make ends meet. She also chose to ignore the knowledge that he was not paying off his debts because he preferred to spend his money on other unrelated, often frivolous luxuries, expenses that only compounded his financial stress.

How many times do we venture forward in a romantic relationship even though we know in our "inner true-north" that something isn't right? How often do we ignore that sense of knowing for fear of disappointing the other? We may hold our tongue and choose not to speak our truth in an effort to avoid hurting another person, thereby colluding in the manufacture of a ticking time bomb. Consider the following statements spoken by various clients:

- My husband and I married when I was twenty-six and he was fifty-one. Keith was twenty-five years older and financially well off. He said that he wanted to someday be a father, but I didn't want to have children. Instead, I wanted to travel, and I figured Keith would, too. After we married, he became insistent on having children. I eventually caved and said yes. I feel like a single mother.

- I don't have a business mind, but my girlfriend does. When we got married I liked that she understood business and finance. I was willing to stay home and take care of things there while she earned the big paycheck. Now I resent the fact that she is so involved in the business and does not see how I matter.

- When I was in medical school Silvia told me that she would continue to have a business career even after I started practicing. I knew that once my practice took off, we wouldn't need her income, but I didn't say anything because I thought she would see how being at home could be just as fulfilling. This has become a point of contention for both of us. I want her to stay home, but she continues to work.

In the final example above, Silvia openly stated that being a stay-at-home doctor's wife was not something she wanted. Ben avoided having this difficult conversation with his wife about what he wanted. As their relationship progressed it caused major resentment on both sides. The spoken agreement between Ben and Silvia was that she would work and he would continue in his medical practice. The silent arrangement (for Ben) began when he avoided having the tough conversation about wanting something different.

How many relationships begin with the ominous belief that *I don't care for his/her friends but once we're together he/she will drop them*? A lot, that's how many. I see it all the time and it always causes problems later on. The simple truth is that when we remain committed to blind hope or desire, we ensure the eventual demise of our relationship. Even worse, by deluding ourselves with our own blind hopes and/or desires, we risk losing not only our relationship with our significant other, but also our relationship with our self.

WHAT I WOULDN'T DO FOR YOU

On several levels we often know more than we think we do when we make (or ignore) important decisions with potential partners. But what issues are at the core of these self-defeating patterns?

As it turns out, Shawn grew up with an overbearing mother and an emotionally weak father. His father often complained about how controlling, unfair, and emotionally withholding Shawn's mother was. Shawn's male role model was a man who saw himself as a victim, helpless to overcome his wife's controlling nature. It was not surprising, then, for Shawn to complain about the domineering woman in his life (Kelly). Of course, his complaints were somewhat ironic since throughout his life he had chronically placed himself at the behest of any number of domineering women. His pattern of financial sabotage kept him "stuck" in the role of victim and guaranteed his dependence on women.

As a result, Kelly was forced to bear the lion's share of the work, and that did not change over time. Nevertheless, Kelly chose to ignore and/ or not ask for the vital information that she needed. Being in *a* relationship was more important to Kelly than being in a *healthy* relationship.

Kelly, on the other hand, is the kind of person who needs to control and refuses to be controlled – at all costs. She grew up with a domineering father and a submissive mother. For years, she witnessed her mother's submissive nature. Kelly made a decision early in life to never submit to any male. Her need to control became a restorative turning of the tables. In fact, she'd even chosen a career in a male-dominated field (construction), rising in the ranks to the level of foreman. On the worksite, she was in charge.

In Shawn and Kelly's relationship the power and control dynamic each of them learned in childhood continued, unabated. Shawn refused to take financial responsibility for himself and in so doing he reveled in his role as victim. Kelly accepted a man who was easy to control, and in so doing reveled in her role as the family power.

The spoken agreement between them called for Shawn to become more financially responsible. The silent arrangement allowed Kelly to retain power and control, and Shawn to endure in the role of victim.

WOULD YOU MARRY YOURSELF OR SOMEONE LIKE YOU?

I often ask my clients if they would marry someone like themselves. The responses that I have received can be quite illuminating:

- *"No I wouldn't marry anyone like myself. I don't like me or the company I keep."*

- *"No, but I would like to be able to answer this question with a yes."*

- *"Yes, no doubt about it. If you had asked me that question some months ago, the answer would have been no. I'm proud to say that now the answer is yes."*

- *"Hmm...that's a tough question."*

- *"I think I make a good prospect, but I would also be aware of the challenges that come with marrying someone like me."*

- *"I would definitely marry someone like myself because then we'd be in constant agreement on everything – boring but a good thing!"*

- *"Yes, well...No, I'm not sure."*

- *"Yes, I like me and there's nothing to not like about me."*

- *"Knowing what I now know, I would definitely NOT want to marry someone like me.*

- *"Wow that is a loaded question. I believe the answer is yes. I am motivated, self-reliant, and able to face most challenges that fall into my lap. I am occasionally a bit selfish, but I am loyal beyond what one would expect is humanly possible, and I would move the world to help my family."*

- *"What kind of question is that?"*

- *"Um...I...think...so?"*

- *"Absolutely NOT! I think I'm great and all, but I could never live with myself. I think I'm too emotionally intense for there to be two of us in a marriage. Although maybe I could marry me now, in my late forties. I have mellowed a ton."*

- *"Yes, I would marry someone like me because I am strong, intelligent, and I have a sense of humor and a positive outlook on life."*

So, how would you answer this question? Would you marry yourself? If so, why?

If no, why not? After you've answered this question, I suggest you proceed to the following two exercises. The questions in these exercises are meant as a guide to help you and your partner assess the level of awareness and you and your relationship. Discussing issues that arise before they become larger threats to your relationship will go a long way to ensuring the health and longevity of your connection.

EXERCISE #1 SELF-INTROSPECTION:

Below you will find several questions that you may or may not have previously asked of yourself or your partner. When you are finished writing down your thoughts, you may wish to share your inventory with your partner. Remind yourself that your answers are meant to help you learn about each other and to practice open and honest communication in your relationship. In Chapter Fourteen, "Restoring the Relationship," we'll discuss how to put this introspection to practice.

1. Would you marry yourself or someone like you?

   _____

   _____

   _____

   _____

2. What information do I already know about my partner?

   _____

   _____

   _____

   _____

3. What information do I still need to know about my partner?

   _____

   _____

   _____

   _____

4. If I am choosing to ignore information that I already have, what is it?

   _____

   _____

   _____

   _____

5. Do I really like the person that he/she is? If not, why do I remain with this person?

   _____

   _____

_____

_____

6. What do I like about him/her?

_____

_____

_____

_____

7. What do I dislike about him/her?

_____

_____

_____

_____

8. Do I love the person he/she is?

_____

_____

_____

_____

9. What do I love about him/her?

_____

_____

_____

_____

EXERCISE #2 THE GIFTS OF OUR RELATIONSHIP

1. What strengths/weaknesses do I bring to the relationship?

_____

_____

_____

_____

2. What strengths/weaknesses does my partner bring to the relationship?

_____

_____

_____

_____

3. What do I most value in relationships?

_____

_____

_____

_____

4. What does my partner most value in relationships?

_____

_____

_____

_____

CHAPTER 14

RESTORING THE RELATIONSHIP

The results of any traumatic experience, such as abuse, can only be resolved by experiencing, articulating, and judging every facet of the original experience within a process of careful therapeutic disclosure.

— Alice Miller

In therapy, both individuals must show up for the work and commit to it, providing equal effort. It's important to realize that individual emotional strengths might make for disparate paths along the way, but an agreed upon outcome and timeframe must be established, and both partners must buy into that plan.

BRINGING DOWN THE DEFENSES

Discord in relationships is inevitable and, actually, a part of any healthy relationship. Learning how to manage that discord goes a long way toward thriving within the relational ups and downs and building intra- and inter-emotional muscle. However, each relationship has unique forms of discord, so there is no one-size-fits-all therapy protocol. What works for one individual or couple may not work for another

In Chapter Three, "Your Relational Currency," we explored Katie and Chuck's relationship. Katie was enamored with Chuck's lithe social ease and his ability to make conversation in any business or social realm. Chuck's established financial success and social standing were very appealing to her. Several years later, Katie seemed to have forgotten that Chuck's success in business was what helped to make him so attractive to her.

For Katie, as is often the case in relationships, aspects of a partner's personality and behaviors that were initially adored gradually became facets of disdain. If Katie and Chuck were ever going to find their way back to financial and sexual fidelity, they would both have to address this issue. Furthermore, both would need to shoulder the burden of therapy. This last point is of the utmost significance. As I guided them toward their personal and joint recovery, I was strongly reminded of my own work in learning how to communicate and compromise in relationships.

At one point during my therapy my therapist asked me, "Do you want to be right or do you want to be happy?" She was trying to convey to me that I didn't always have the luxury of being right, but I did (always) have the opportunity to be happy. Of course, our need for control (to be right) is often driven by underlying anxieties stemming from childhood. And some of us are more highly defensive and committed to "being right" than others. This fact raises a natural therapeutic question: What about the current situation or person is causing a need to be defensive? Is this his/her old inner narrative from childhood screaming "You're not good enough?" Or is there some other, much more valid reason why a partner is not willing to compromise?

In Chapter Seven "Icarus Revisited" we explored the concept of gaslighting. To summarize, gaslighting is a form of psychological abuse and intimidation used to disorient a person's sense of reality. I am aware of this manipulation and keep my antennae open particularly when narcissistic partners are endeavoring to win back the potential loss of something or someone valued. Vulnerable partners or spouses may not be strong enough to withstand the tentacles of the abuser but will, however, register resistance in the therapy process.

THE BUILDING BLOCKS OF CONNECTION

In one of our sessions I asked Chuck to remind himself and Katie what he initially found so adoring about her. And I suggested he include some tenderness in his delivery, which he did.

"I loved your quick wit, your ability to hold your own in negotiations with male business associates, and the fact that you weren't needy. You could run circles around me in business. No woman I had ever met could do what you did AND look sexy."

Katie was less agitated than she had been in earlier sessions but was still prickly enough to counter with a jibe.

"Oh, come on Chuck! You only loved my body and the fact that it was yours!"

Chuck acknowledged that he enjoyed Katie's looks, and that was a major factor in why he'd pursued her. She was ten years younger than he was, and he'd liked that. Their relational currency, as we discussed in Chapter Three, was *I'll provide the salary if you provide the looks.*

Katie turned to address me, but then she turned her attention back to Chuck, softening significantly.

"I believe that you don't find me attractive anymore. This isn't easy for me to say. I'm so hurt by that, and I'm utterly furious at you, Chuck, for your affairs. I don't trust you anymore, but I'm worried that you've been doing what you've been doing because I'm no longer attractive."

All of Katie's earlier venom seemed to melt into fear, pain, and shame with this statement. This was the vulnerability that she had always worked so hard to mask and the one exchange between Katie and Chuck that became the crucial factor to saving their marriage. After this, their progress amazed even me. In therapy Chuck began to address his sexual addiction. He committed to doing individual therapy as well as attending my men's sex addiction group. He followed through with twelve-step "S" meetings and found a sponsor with whom he kept in close contact. Several weeks later he agreed to a formal disclosure session in which he detailed his entire history of sexual infidelity. In the process, he held himself accountable for his behavior. He then shared with Katie about the work he was committed to continuing for his personal recovery and for their relationship.

For her part, Katie attended meetings for partners of sex addicts and immersed herself in her own personal work. She connected with a sponsor who helped Katie maintain her accountability for her behavior and recovery.

Finally, they attended couple's counseling on a regular basis, and while not all of their sessions went as well as the ones described above, they were able to significantly improve their style of communication. By learning to tap into their more vulnerable selves, they became less assaultive toward each other. Ever so slowly, Katie softened her approach and Chuck became less shaming and one-up in his communication style. Eventually they were able to restore the connection that had almost disappeared from their marriage.

THE PRICE OF ENTRY

In order to ensure the highest degree of authentic relating we must learn to take responsibility for ourselves and our actions. Consider the following questions for introspection:

- What do I value in a relationship?

- What are my needs and wants in a relationship?

- Do I ask for what I need?

- Is my partner able to give me what I need and want?

- Am I willing to own my own reality and not project it onto others?

- Will I be compassionate toward myself as well as those around me?

- Do I trust myself?

- Am I willing to trust another?

- Am I capable of being emotionally available in a relationship? Can I say the same about my partner?

Q. <u>WHAT DO I VALUE IN A RELATIONSHIP?</u>

To improve our understanding of the motivations we have behind the decisions we make, it helps to pinpoint what we really value in a relationship. Our head might say we want connection, but if our past has produced a pattern of unavailable partners, perhaps the answer is slightly different. Recognizing what we truly value in a relationship is the first step in understanding why we may become disappointed time and again. A friend of mine once said to me, "It's amazing. I don't believe that there are really healthy women out there. They bring such drama into the relationship!" I held my tongue, as I've long made a promise never to offer therapeutic advice or feedback to anyone who has not asked for it.

But what was clear to me is that my friend chooses women who validate his cynical view of the world as being self-serving and an ultimate let-down. He will either come to terms with his own self-righteous patterns in selection of women (not to mention employment, as all of his jobs seemed to terminate with his being right and the boss being wrong), or he would be doomed to a life of relational failure. It seems to me that he values being self-righteous more than he values being in a healthy relationship.

Q. WHAT ARE MY NEEDS AND WANTS IN A RELATIONSHIP?

This question is perhaps the most essential in securing the healthy and emotionally connected outcomes in *all* relationships, be they business, social, romantic, or friendship. A need is something we have to have. Its absence would constitute a deal-breaker in any relationship. A want is something that would be nice to have, but it's not a deal-breaker if it's not there. A partner who never argues with my point of view, however unlikely this is, would be a want, for example. I recognize that this is a want and not a need, and I accept the fact that it is likely never to happen. Oh well…

If there is any hesitation about putting something on the needs list, then it belongs on the wants list. A former client with whom I worked expressed that this time around she would only marry a rich man. This was a need in that she would not even consider love, compatibility, connection, or common spiritual beliefs before wealth. So be it. That need superseded all else. I probably don't need to tell you that she was in therapy to sort out why she was struggling with her current relationship – an affair she was having with a not-yet-divorced and emotionally unavailable man. I held no judgment about her first-order decree. I also knew that a healthy relationship based on love would likely elude her for quite some time.

Q. DO I ASK FOR WHAT I NEED?

Simple enough, right? Wrong! Knowing what we need and being bold enough to ask for it are two different issues. We must be willing to uphold our needs; otherwise our vision for what we want for ourselves dissolves into thin air. This takes practice and is certainly easier said than done. It also takes an understanding of what a boundary is and how to maintain one. A boundary states what action I am willing to take in order to take care of myself. An example is, "In order to take care of myself I will not allow another person to verbally abuse me. I will ask him/her to stop and if they continue I will disengage from the conversation." Or, "Please do not call me if you are active in your addiction." Stating a boundary is the easy part, holding a boundary is yet another. Most importantly, we must be willing to take care of ourselves even in the face of resistance from another.

Q. IS MY PARTNER ABLE TO GIVE ME WHAT I NEED AND WANT?

To know what we need and want and be prepared to stand our ground is the first major hurdle in a relationship. Is our partner capable of or willing to offer that which we ask for? This is where Chapter Thirteen, "Spoken Agreements and Silent Arrangements," comes in. We all but ensure our relational demise when we agree to something but have little to no intention of following through. Every time we move the line away from what we need and move it toward what we will accept, we guarantee disappointment and most likely resentment in our relationship. Knowing what our partner is capable of and willing to do lends clarity to the outcome of any relationship.

Q. AM I WILLING TO OWN MY OWN REALITY INSTEAD OF PROJECTING IT ONTO OTHERS?

Step four in any twelve-step recovery program is to look inward and make a "searching and fearless moral inventory of ourselves." Even people not in recovery can benefit from this, as it teaches us that we are responsible for our own thoughts, actions, and emotions. Our willingness to hold ourselves accountable instead of projecting blame onto others is a significant step toward establishing genuine connections. This also helps us to cut down on the depth and number of resentments we formulate and hold. Of course, a fearless and searching moral inventory is easier said than done. If you are in addiction recovery, then working with a sponsor on your fourth step will be helpful. Those who do not attend twelve-step meetings can find support in a therapist or a trusted and wise other, someone who will help you see what you need to see, not just what you want to see.

Recovery means living life on life's terms and not living it through the lens of how we want it to be just to suit our own desires. At times this means disappointing ourselves and/or another. Recovery demands that we be willing to do this in order to live a healthy and fulfilled life. Meeting the demands of life is a formidable if not herculean challenge for many of us. More difficult yet, is our basic challenge to set and meet our own demands and realities; these begin only when we are willing to be honest with ourselves. The rigorous honesty demanded of ourselves is no less necessary when in a relationship.

Q. WILL I BE COMPASSIONATE TOWARD MYSELF AS WELL AS THOSE AROUND ME?

I addressed shame in Chapter Two, "Sex, Shame, and Anger." Children shamed in childhood learn to use unhealthy defense mechanisms to outwardly become invulnerable. The defenses they construct around their wounded soul serve as protection from external wounding; unfortunately, they also shield the individual from his or her own sense of worthiness and lovability. Therefore, compassion for self and anybody else ceases to exist. When we process and reduce the level of toxic shame (which, by its definition wasn't ours to begin with but was handed down to us in a dysfunctional family system) we can begin to feel humility for ourselves and others. The gift of processed shame is humility and compassion. When we learn how to trust ourselves, we can begin to trust others. We also experience what I call *the big thaw* – a warming of our frozen emotions, which we purposely sealed off and denied to avoid reliving our childhood loneliness and fear. When we begin to treat ourselves with compassion and kindness we dissolve the cloud of shame that surrounds us.

Q. DO I TRUST MYSELF?

Many therapy clients initially express an inability to trust themselves (or another) due to betrayal by a trusted caregiver in childhood or disclosure by their partner of sexual and financial infidelity. This makes perfect sense. A history of learned experiences has altered these individuals' ability to accurately discern who is trustworthy. More importantly, relearning how to trust is not easy. Rebuilding the capacity to decipher and assess truth is perhaps the most important thing one can do in terms of restoring a sense of self.

Partners of sex addicts who have knowingly or unknowingly endured deceit and lies need a new trust set-point, not one defined by the yet-to-be-delivered promises of the cheating partner. To this end I often encourage my clients to write a truth on a piece of paper and label it with the date and time. I tell them that they can only write a truth down if it is an *absolute truth* and you know it in your "knower." This means only writing down that which you know and believe to be true beyond a shadow of a doubt. For example, "I know that I was lied to by my partner this weekend because I caught him in a lie," "I feel angry about the conversation with…," or "I am confident that I did a good job on this project at work, and I feel proud of myself for…."

As we practice with learning how to listen to our own gut instinct our resolve may crumble, for example, if we are experiencing gaslighting by an addict's story. It is natural to question our own perception from time to time, anyway.

By writing your truth and time-stamping it, you have a touchstone to reference when doubt and mistrust creep in. If you are a partner dealing with infidelity and you know that your spouse or the addict has lied to you, it is common to doubt your perspective due to lies told by the addict and/or an eroding sense of inner-strength. By repeating this exercise you can begin to build a foundation of consistent truths, helping you to learn how to trust yourself and eventually use your instincts in assessing others and their behavior. This leads me to the next point.

Q. AM I WILLING TO TRUST ANOTHER?

Not until he or she has earned your trust! Trust is earned, not granted, and doesn't happen until such time trustworthiness is consistently demonstrated.

Q. AM I CAPABLE OF BEING EMOTIONALLY AVAILABLE IN A RELATIONSHIP? CAN I SAY THE SAME ABOUT MY PARTNER?

Building connection begins with being honest about what we need and want in a relationship. It is also a product of trust in our self and another person. However, the key to building connection is boundaries with oneself and with others. This is perhaps one of the most difficult responsibilities of being in a relationship.

Without question, healthy boundaries are the hallmark of a healthy union. Knowing where I end and you begin is fundamental for any interaction, especially a romantic connection. Unfortunately, many couples have difficulty implementing this key element. As discussed earlier in Chapter One, "Sex, Love, and Attachment," people who struggle with the concept of connection and intimacy do so because early attachment was lacking or was built around distancing rather than connecting. For the sex addict, relationship building tends to be overlooked in return for sexual manipulation and conquest. Sex and love addicts by their nature tend to exhibit weak or failed boundaries, since sex is typically enlisted in the service of securing attachment, love, or approval. As such, building emotional muscle, tolerating dis-ease, and reducing shame are hallmarks of recovery.

In my work with sex and love addiction I have often heard these two phrases: "I completely lose myself in order to be loved by him/her." Or "I thought that if I could just become everything he was looking for or needed, then he wouldn't go outside the relationship." In order for true recovery to take shape, these core beliefs will have to change. In other words, healing from infidelity and addiction begins with rigorous honesty and introspective work. Starting with the first step of self-love and friendship (where it may have never existed before) is not only healthy but necessary for a new experience of true connection.

EPILOGUE

Sex has come to be used as some kind of a drug: in order to escape reality, to forget about problems, to relax. And like all drugs, this is a harmful and destructive practice.

– Paulo Coelho, Eleven Minutes

It would be nice to say that sex addiction is on the decline and that sexual and financial exploitation disappeared along with the dot.com era. However, neither of those statements is true. Whether sex addiction, as a diagnosis, will ever be included in the go-to reference of psychiatric illnesses known as the Diagnostic and Statistical Manual of Mental Disorders (DSM) remains to be seen. I would like to say that its inclusion doesn't matter, but that would also not be true. That said, at its naissance, Alcoholics Anonymous (AA) was no more welcome at the medical table of believers than sex addiction is now, and AA has nevertheless saved the lives of countless alcoholics. Programs focused on recovering from sexual addiction do the same.

In this day and age of statistical analysis and factual findings, no one has managed to locate the Holy Grail of proof that sex addiction is real, but that doesn't mean it's not. Apparently, what is missing is the research to indicate proof-positive outcomes. Either way, try telling the scores of sex addicts, along with their partners and their families, that their sex addiction isn't a real issue!

While some people may argue that sex addiction is some type of myth, those of us who work in the therapeutic trenches now see sex addiction and the accompanying devastation walk over our thresholds and into our offices at an increasingly alarming rate. The omnipresence of the Internet has created what we know as the "Triple-A Engine" effect: accessibility, affordability, and anonymity.[1]

For the narcissistic and pathological, as goes sex and money, so goes the potential for sexual and financial exploitation. As long as money and sex retain their prioritized value in relationships (and not always in that order) an addict's need for power, intensity, and control will follow. As such, the two will assuredly preserve their commoditized roles in bedrooms and boardrooms alike.

I've learned a lot about working with addiction over the years and more when it comes to sex addiction. I wrote earlier in the book that this work is not for the faint of heart. Many of the clients that I have had the honor of helping have endured experiences in childhood that no child should know. Still others have tolerated conditions as children that they now see were less than nurturing or blatant abuse. Neither they nor I can change their past. However, together we have been able to rewrite their future. "The past only informs who you have become," I say. "It does not dictate who you have yet to be." The ways in which sex has been solicited to hide pain, fear, loneliness, anger, guilt, and shame varies by the individual. No two paths of sex addiction are identical.

There are the individuals who are forced into recovery upon accidental disclosure or reprisal from a loved one. At some point or another in the process, some addicts comprehend the reality of their manipulation and rage. It becomes more than they can handle. This moment of absolute humility becomes their wakeup call and a redemptive moment of true transformation. For some others, this never happens, which is sad. But it doesn't stop me from trying.

I like working with the complexities of trauma, sex addiction and financial exploitation. How trauma is manifested in each individual and the ways in which that trauma is reenacted through a person's arousal template is fascinating not only to me but to my clients. I remember several sessions in which my clients have gasped upon discovery of the incredible nature of their unconscious reenactment. It is an honor to share in my client's recovery journeys. I cherish that honor, and I hope to continue guiding many clients out of their addiction into their well-deserved joy.

I also enjoy the challenge of remaining neutral in my work with couples. "Whose side am I on?" they ask, as if they might somehow trap me. My standard answer is: "I'm on the side of health. I'm rooting for the two of you to align together against the addiction, the trauma, and the need for usurpative power and control in the relationship. I am working for the relationship."

My clients are always the courageous ones. They are the brave ones who continue to show up, do the work, and remain committed to change. I won't say that all of the individuals and couples who seek therapy have positive and productive outcomes, but what I can say is that most do. It would be selfish to say that their success has been due to my guidance, even though sometimes that might be true. Without question, however, the lion's share of the transformation occurs deep within them – by their choice.

"What stirs your soul and makes your heart sing, I ask?" Not all clients have the answer, but most are compelled to find out.

I began *For Love and Money* with a quote on how we love and connect to another person. It is only fitting that I end the book with a quote about a search for sex, love, and true connection. Paulo Coelho's *Eleven Minutes* is a novel about a young woman named Maria who at a young age believes that she will never find true love. Rather than look inward at her fear, she chooses a life that leads her down a lurid path of dark, sexual intensity. The intensity nearly consumes her before she experiences an awakening. Coelho's Maria is everyman and everywoman – the addict who values the magical clout of sex and money to escape his or her own soul.

> *"It took me a long time to learn that the coming together of two bodies is more than a response to certain physical stimuli or to the survival instinct. Sex is a manifestation of a spiritual energy called love. Sex means, above all, having the courage to experience your own paradoxes, individuality, and willingness to surrender."*

> — *Paulo Coelho, Eleven Minutes*

ADDENDUM ON ATTACHMENT

John Bowlby's and Mary Ainsworth's individual paths and collective efforts in the field of child development and attachment research paved the way for subsequent and seminal research delivering differential theories on the sequelae of attachment classifications.

In, *The Origins of Attachment Theory: John Bowlby and Mary Ainsworth,* Dr. Inge Bretheron, a former student of Mary Ainsworth and now a distinguished professor and noted researcher in internal working models of attachment relationships had this to say:

> *"... More recently, interest (in) adult attachments has broadened to encompass marital relationships (Weiss, 1982, 1991) and has taken a further upsurge with work by Shaver and Hazan (1988), who translated Ainsworth's infant attachment patterns into adult patterns, pointing out that adults who describe themselves as secure, avoidant, or ambivalent with respect to romantic relationships report differing patterns of parent-child relationships in their families of origin."* [1]

Several distinct paths of attachment research grew out of Bowlby and Ainsworth's seminal work. One such path led by Dr. Mary Main, a former student of Mary Ainsworth, produced *The Adult Attachment Interview* (George, Kaplan, & Main, 1985, 1996), an interview procedure for assessing adults' narrative of self-identification, prevention and protection from perceived dangers. In particular these perceived dangers are tied to intimate relationships. The work that grew out of Ainsworth's research, according to Drs., Bartholomew and Shaver *Methods of Assessing Adult Attachment: Do They Converge?*, emphasized interview measures and behavioral observations.

The second, independent path of research included the collective work of Drs. Cindy Hazan, Cornell University and Phillip Shaver, University of California, Davis, who were investigating adolescent and adult loneliness. Hazan and Shaver were personality/ social psychologists, and according to Bartholomew and Shaver, "their work was quickly assimilated by other such psychologists, who tend to think in terms of personality traits and social interactions, be interested in normal subject populations, prefer simple questionnaire measures, study relatively large samples, and focus on adult social relationships, including friendships, dating relationships, and marriages."[2]

Bringing the two divergent, yet similar paths together, Drs. Bartholomew and Horowitz proposed an expanded model of adult attachment (Figure 1.) that included two forms of avoidance. To assess this model, they used a self-report measure of experiences in close relationships in general (by revising Hazan and Shaver's measure) as well as two interviews, one focusing on childhood experiences (along the lines of the AAI) and the other focusing on peer relationships, including friendships and romantic relationships (Bartholomew & Horowitz, 1991).[3]

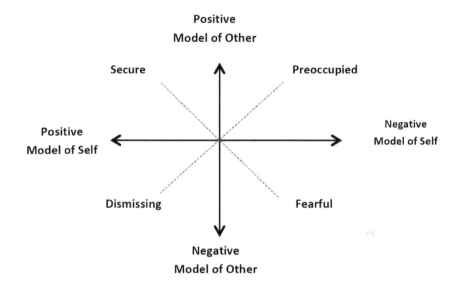

Figure 1. Two-dimensional four-category model of adult attachment.

Earlier, in 1964, Rudolph Schaffer and Peggy Emerson theorized that children could direct their attention to any available person. However, they noted that by the sixth or seventh month of life most normal infants selectively direct their attention to one person. "It is from this particular person that they seek proximity and from whom they object to being separated." [4] Thirty years later, in 1994, Drs., Hazan and Shaver, went on to hypothesize that our early displays of attachment are the same systems that govern our adult romantic relational interactions. What Hazan and Shaver specifically found in their work was a distribution of adult attachment categories. Those being, "55% secure, 25% avoidant, and 20% anxious/ambivalent that has subsequently been replicated in many studies in several different countries (e.g. Feeney & Noller, 1990; Hazan & Shaver, 1987: Mikulincer, Florian, & Tolmacz, 1990).

The list of preeminent researchers that include Bowlby and Ainsworth and continue up to today is extensive and would be too plentiful in numbers to include here. However, in 1987, a direction of research was continued by Drs. Hazan and Shaver. They hypothesized that adult romantic love is an attachment process similar to and consistent with the biosocial process formed in earlier life between infants and their caregivers. Their work centered on the research developed by Bowlby and Ainsworth, et al., regarding development of attachment bonds in infancy and were translated into terms appropriate to adult romantic love.

The work of Hazan and Shaver focused on secure, anxious, and avoidant attachment styles, three patterns identified by Ainsworth, Blehar, Waters, & Wall (1978) in their studies of infant-caregiver attachment which is of particular importance when discussing attachment styles, emotional avoidance/ anxiety, and sex addiction.[5]

Later in 1998 Drs. Brennan, Clark, and Shaver expanded on work previously conducted by Drs. Bartholomew and Horowitz (1991) with their publication of the Experiences in Close Relationship Questionnaire (ECR) indicating that "individual differences in attachment can be measured along two roughly orthogonal dimensions: attachment-related *anxiety* and *avoidance*. A person's position on the anxiety dimension indicates the degree to which he or she worries that a partner will not be available and responsive in times of need. "A person's position on the avoidance dimension indicates the extent to which he or she distrusts relationship partners' good will and strives to maintain behavioral independence and emotional distance from partners."[6]

Drs. Fraley, Waller, and Brennan (2000) expanded on Brennan, Clark, and Shaver's (1998) Experiences in Close Relationships (ECR) questionnaire with a revised update (ECR-R) (Figure 2). The two axes of anxiety and avoidance were expanded "to assess individual differences with respect to attachment-related anxiety (i.e., the extent to which people are insecure vs. secure about the extent to which their partner's availability and responsiveness) and attachment-related avoidance (i.e., the extent to which people are uncomfortable being close to others vs. secure depending on others)."[7]

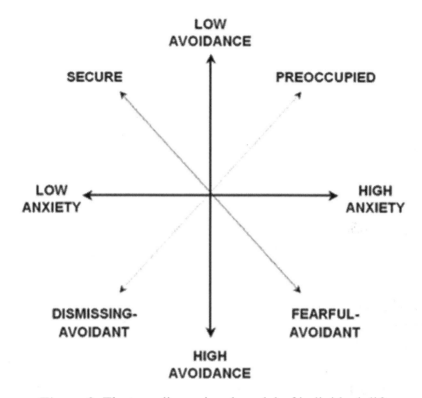

Figure 2. The two-dimensional model of individual differences in adult attachment.

To date there is a need for more empirically driven studies measuring adult romantic attachment, but much work has been already been accomplished from the original work of Bowlby and Ainsworth. Consider the following summary in *Romantic Love Conceptualized as an Attachment Process*, by Drs. Hazan and Shaver (1986):

> *"Love and loneliness are emotional processes that serve biological functions. Attachment theory portrays them in that light and urges us to go beyond simpler and less theoretically integrative models involving concepts such as attitude (e.g., Rubin,1973) and physiological*

arousal (Berscheid & Walster, 1974). For that reason, the attachment approach seems worth pursuing even if future study reveals (as it almost certainly will) that adult romantic love requires additions to or alterations in attachment theory. It would not be surprising to find that adult love is more complex than infant-caretaker attachment, despite fundamental similarities. "[8]

Hazan and Shaver continued to explore Bowlby's ideas but did so from the context of adult romantic relationships. They went on to say that the emotional bonds that develop between adult romantic partners arise to some degree from the same early attachment behavioral system about which Bowlby postulated. Both investigators went on to research and publish extensively on observed parallels between the infant caregiver attachment behavioral system and the adult attachment behavioral system and hypothesizing that the latter just may be an outcropping of the former. Adult romantic love, they argued, "is a property of the attachment behavioral system, as well as the motivational systems that give rise to caregiving and sexuality."[9]

Mikulincer and Shaver (2003, 2007) proposed that a person's location in the two-dimensional conceptual space defined by attachment anxiety and avoidance reflects both the person's sense of attachment security and the ways in which he or she deals with threats and distress. People who score low on these dimensions are generally secure and tend to employ constructive and effective affect-regulation strategies. Their ability to handle both the *intra* and *inter* psychic distress allows for the emotional and relational flexibility thereby ensuring a more successful outcome during times of stressful interaction.

On the other extreme are those who score high on both the attachment anxiety and the avoidant attachment dimension. These individuals suffer from attachment insecurities and tend to rely on what Cassidy and Kobak (1988) called *secondary attachment strategies* – deactivating or hyper-activating their attachment system in an effort to cope with threats. Deactivating strategies are employed by those who actively distance, deny attachment needs, and avoid closeness and interdependence in relationships. Those characteristics comprise the Fearful-Avoidant attachment spectrum. As a result of attachment figures who disapprove of and punish closeness and expressions of need or vulnerability these individuals register high anxiety and avoidance in relationships despite desiring to connect and wishing to bond.

Those scoring high on attachment anxiety and low on avoidance tend to rely on hyper-activating strategies – active attempts to achieve closeness and proximity, love and support. However, childhood experience has established that attempts at connection will produce an inconsistent, at times hostile and angry, connection with significant caregivers. "These reactions occur in relationships in which an attachment figure is sometimes responsive but unreliably so, placing the needy person on a partial reinforcement schedule that rewards persistence in proximity-seeking attempts, because they sometimes succeed."[10]

Gurit E. Birnbaum, Israeli psychologist and researcher with the Interdisciplinary Center (IDC) in Herzliya, Israel, has focused her research interests on romantic relationships, human sexuality, and evolutionary psychology. Findings derived from Birnbaum's research with attachment dimensions and sexual and romantic relationships to date illustrate the need for additional understanding of how our attachment and sexual systems mutually influence each other at different stages of relationship development.

Consider the following work by Birnbaum:

> More avoidant individuals, in contrast, feel uncomfortable with the closeness inherently involved in sexual interactions and, therefore, tend to detach sexuality from psychological intimacy (Mikulincer & Shaver, 2007; Shaver Mikulincer, 2006).This detached stance may account for diverse avoidance related sexual behaviors and motives, such as experiencing sexual fantasies in which they and the object of their fantasies are represented as interpersonally distant and alienated

(Birnbaum, 2007b), engaging in less-frequent sexual activities with relationship partners (Brassard, Shaver, & Lussier 2007), reliance on the solitary sexual activity of masturbation, engaging in emotion-free sex (e.g., one-night stands; sex with casual partners), and having sex for relationship-irrelevant, self-enhancing reasons (see the reviews by Cooper et al., 2006; Mikulincer & Shaver, 2007). When more avoidant people do have sex with their romantic partners, they tend to experience relatively strong feelings of estrangement and alienation and display low levels of physical affection (Birnbaum & Reis, 2006; Birnbaum et al., 2006; Birnbaum, 2007a). Overall, more avoidant individuals seem to have a sex life relatively devoid of affectional bonding, even within the context of ongoing romantic relationships. "[11]

The field of attachment and adult relationships vis-à-vis sexual and emotional behavioral systems is experiencing exciting developments due to joint technological and psychological advances. At the same time cultural mores are shifting and redefining our individual "need" for relationship. In a world that has produced digital communication, virtual sex and relationships, and holographic incarnations we are on the threshold of a newer realm and future meaning of attachment. With collective global research being forged on many fronts, it is clear that the field of attachment is experiencing a psychodynamic as well dynamic paradigm shift.

---

[1] Inge Bretherton, "The Origins of Attachment Theory: John Bowlby and Mary Ainsworth," Developmental Psychology 28 (1992), 759-775.

(http://www.psychology.sunysb.edu/attachment/online/inge_origins. pdf).

[2] American Institute of CPAs, *AICPA Survey: Finances Causing Rifts for American Couples,* http://www.aicpa.org/Press/PressReleases/2012/ Pages/Finances-Causing-Rifts-for-American-Couples.aspx (May 4, 2012), Accessed: August 1, 2012.

[3] K. Bartholomew, L.M. Horowitz, "Attachment styles among young adults: A test of a four category model." *Journal of Personality and Social Psychology* 61 (1991): 226-244.

[4] H.R. Schaffer, P.E. Emerson, "The development of social attachments in infancy," *Monographs of the Society for Research in Child Development,* (1994).

[5] J.L. Zapf, J. Greiner, J. Carroll, "Attachment Styles and Male Sex Addiction," *Sexual Addiction & Compulsivity* 15 (2008): 158–175.

[6] M. Mikulincer, P.R. Shaver, "An attachment perspective on psychopathology," *World Psychiatry.* 11:1 (2012), 11–15, Accessed: July 29, 2012.

[7] T. Ein-Dor, M. Mikulincer, G. Doron, P.R. Shaver, "The attachment paradox: How can so many of us (the insecure ones) have no adaptive advantages?," *Perspectives on Psychological Science,* 5 (2010), 123.

[8] C. Hazan, P.R. Shaver, "Romantic love conceptualized as an attachment process," *Journal of Personality and Social Psychology,* 52:3 (1987), 511-524.

[9] Hazen and Shaver (1987)

[10] J. Cassidy, R.R. Kobak, as quoted in M. Mikulincer, P.R. Shaver, "An attachment perspective on psychopathology," *World Psychiatry.* 11:1 (2012), 11–15, Accessed: July 29, 2012.

[11] Gurit E. Birnbaum, "Bound to interact: The divergent goals and complex interplay of attachment and sex within romantic relationships," *Journal of Social and Personal Relationships, 27,* (2010): 245-252, Accessed November 2, 2012.

ENDNOTES

PREFACE:

[1] A physical commodity is an actual product that is sold or traded. There are two types of commodities: hard and soft. Hard commodities include crude oil, iron ore, gold, and silver, and they have a long shelf-life. Soft commodities are agricultural products such as soybeans, rice, and wheat. They are considered soft commodities because they have a limited shelf-life. Commodities have to be similar and interchangeable to be traded. For example, soybeans from one provider, country, or market should be of the same quality as soybeans from another provider, etc. Newer contracts such as electricity, bonds, and currencies are also traded as commodities in global markets.

[2] "Corporate raiders use tactics such as taking a company private, thwarting a spin-off, calling for a new board of directors or arranging a sale of assets. For a factual depiction of the era, read *Den of Thieves* by Pulitzer Prize winner, James B. Steward, about the insider trading scandals and the four biggest names on Wall Street -- Michael Milken, Ivan Boesky, Martin Siegel, and Dennis Levine, who made that happen.

[3] Four World Trade Center was a nine-story office building that stood in the shadows of the taller and more widely known "twin towers." Many people are unaware that there were in fact seven towers (of varying

heights) within the World Trade Center complex; not just the two twin towers that fell following the terrorist attack on New York.

[4] **Daniel Kahneman** has integrated insights from psychology into economics, thereby laying the foundation for a new field of research. Kahneman's main findings concern decision-making under uncertainty, where he has demonstrated how human decisions may systematically depart from those predicted by standard economic theory. Together with Amos Tversky (deceased in 1996), he has formulated prospect theory as an alternative, that better accounts for observed behavior. Kahneman has also discovered how human judgment may take heuristic shortcuts that systematically depart from basic principles of probability. His work has inspired a new generation of researchers in economics and finance to enrich economic theory using insights from cognitive psychology into intrinsic human motivation.

Vernon Smith has laid the foundation for the field of experimental economics. He has developed an array of experimental methods, setting standards for what constitutes a reliable laboratory experiment in economics. In his own experimental work, he has demonstrated the importance of alternative market institutions, e.g., how the revenue expected by a seller depends on the choice of auction method. Smith has also spearheaded "wind-tunnel tests", where trials of new, alternative market designs – e.g., when deregulating electricity markets – are carried out in the lab before being implemented in practice. His work has been instrumental in establishing experiments as an essential tool in empirical economic analysis." Nobel Prizes and Laureates, http://www.nobelprize.org/nobel_prizes/economic sciences/laureates/2002/press.html, (October 9, 2002), Accessed: July 2, 2012.

CHAPTER 1
SEX, LOVE AND ATTACHMENT

[1] Brodie, Richard. "John Bowlby: The Father of Attachment Theory," http://www.childdevelopmentmedia.com/john-bowlby-the-father-of-attachment-theory.html, Accessed: March 12, 2013.

2 Mary Salter Ainsworth, "Object Relations, Dependency, and Attachment: A Theoretical Review of the Infant-Mother Relationship," *Child Development,* http://www.psychology.sunysb.edu/attachment/online/attach_depend.pdf, 1969, Accessed: January 4, 2013.

3 Mikulincer, M., Dolev, T., & Shaver, P. R., "Attachment-Related Strategies During Thought Suppression: Ironic Rebounds and Vulnerable Self-Representations," *Journal of Personality and Social Psychology,* (2004): 940-956.

4 Fraley, Mikulincer, Shaver, 940-956.

5 Dr. Dylan Selterman, "Attachment Theory: Explaining Relationship 'Styles,'" http://www.scienceofrelationships.com/home/2011/7/15/attachment-theory-explaining- relationship-styles.html, (2011), Accessed: August 29, 2012.

CHAPTER 2
SEX, SHAME AND ANGER

1 Irvin Yalom, *The Gift of Therapy: An Open Letter to a New Generation of Therapists and Their Patients,* (Harper Perennial, 2009), 182.

CHAPTER 3
YOUR RELATIONAL CURRENCY

1 Catherine Hakim, *Erotic Capital: The Power of Attraction in the Boardroom and the Bedroom,* (Basic Books, 2011), 10.

2 Pros and Cons of Controversial Issues, *Prostitution Historical Timeline,* http://prostitution.procon.org/view.resource.php?resourceID=000117 (Dec. 2012), Accessed: December 3, 2012.

3 American Institute of CPAs (AICPA), *AICPA Survey: Finances Causing Rifts for American Couples,* http://www.aicpa.org/press/

pressreleases/2012/pages/finances-causing-rifts-for-american-couples. aspx, (2012), Accessed: January 4, 2013.

CHAPTER 4
EMOTIONAL SCARCITY–SEXUAL SURPLUS

[1] Courtney Comstock, *Deutsche Banker's Kinky Torture Fantasy Ends In Death*, http://www.businessinsider.com/bankers-kinky-torture-fantasy-ends-in-death-2010-8 (August 16, 2010), Accessed: January 6, 2013.

[2] Mike Sullivan and Anthony France, *Girl Kicks away stool and goes without looking back, Important stick to role*, http://www.thesun.co.uk/sol/homepage/news/3096927/Bankers-suicide-text-to-hooker.html, (August 16, 2010), Accessed: January 6, 2012.

[3] Rachel Weiner, *Anthony Weiner details how many women he's had explicit online relationships with*, http://www.washingtonpost.com/politics/anthony-weiner-details-how-many-women-hes-had-online-relationships-with/2013/07/25/c185ad5a-f572-11e2-9434-60440856fadf_story.html (July 25, 2013) Accessed: July 27, 2013.

[4] Gurit E. Birnbaum, "Bound to interact: The divergent goals and complex interplay of attachment and sex within romantic relationships," *Journal of Social and Personal Relationships,* (2010).

[5] Jeff Csatari, *What Your Sex Fantasies Mean, Accessed November 3, 2012 from What Your Sex Fantasies Mean*, http://news.menshealth.com/what-your-sex-fantasies- mean/2011/10/06/ (October 6, 2011) Accessed: June 1, 2012

[6] http://news.menshealth.com/what-your-sex-fantasies-mean/2011/10/06/

[7] John Money, Lovemaps: *Clinical Concepts of Sexual/Erotic Health and Pathology, Paraphilia, and Gender Transposition in Childhood, Adolescence, and Maturity*, (New York: Prometheus Books, 1986).

[8] Patrick Carnes, *Ten Types of Sexual Addiction*, http://www.iitap. com/documents/SDI-R%20The%20Ten%20Types%20-%20Long%20 Version.pdf, (2008), Accessed: February, 2009.

[9] http://www.iitap.com/documents/SDI-R%20The%20Ten%20 Types%20-%20Long%20Version.pdf.

CHAPTER 6
EROTICIZED RAGE

[1] Bessel van der Kolk, "The Compulsion to Repeat the Trauma Re-enactment, Revictimization, and Masochism," *Circumcision Reference Library, Psychiatric Clinics of North America*, (June 1989): 389-411, Accessed: May 3, 2012.

[2] Dr. Patrick Carnes, *Eroticized Rage*, http://www.iitap.com/doc-uments/SDI-R%20Clinical%20Scales%20explanations.pdf, (2008), Accessed: January 15, 2012.

PART II
SEX, MONEY AND POWER

[1] Morris Jastrow, Ph.D., Albert T. Clay, Ph.D., *An Old Babylonian Version of the Gilgamesh Epic*, (Yale University Press, 1920), Accessed on June3, 2012.

[2] Philip Graham Ryken, PhD., *King Solomon: The Temptations of Money, Sex, and Power*, (Crossway Publications, 2010)

[3]   Julie Steinberg, "Wall Street's Cleaner Image Pauses for a Fresh Scandal," *Wall Street Journal online*, August 17, 2012, Accessed July 28, 2013.

CHAPTER 7
ICARUS REVISITED

* While women are equally capable of such, there are a disproportionate number of men who are active in these clusters – certainly in realms of finance, politics, and sports. Despite the fact that at no other time in history have women occupied more positions of authority, these behaviors and personality traits are more commonly found and actively exhibited in the male psyche.

[1]   *Entourage,* Doug Ellin, Home Box Office, 2004. Television.

[2]   *Needs as Personality: Henry Murray*, http://www.wilderdom.com/personality/traits/PersonalityTraitsNeedsHenryMurray.html (July 27, 2004), Accessed: March 23, 2013.

[3]   W. Preston Lear, *The Modern Icarus Complex: A psychoanalytic complex manifest in BASE jumpers and other action sports athletes*, (ProQuest, UMI Dissertations Publishing, 2011), Accessed on December 5, 2012.

[4]   "JPMorgan CEO Jamie Dimon: London Whale Was 'The Stupidest And Most Embarrassing Situation,'" *Huffington Post Online*, April, 11, 2013, Accessed: May 3, 2013

[5]   Andrea Amiel, Alan B. Goldberg, Eric Avram, Michael S. James, "Bernie Madoff 'Can Live With' Fraud Victims' Anger, But Not Family Scorn, He Tells Barbara Walters Exclusively," *ABC News*, Oct. 27, 2011, (http://abcnews.go.com/US/bernie-madoff-live-fraud-victims-anger-familys-tells/story?id=14823108), Accessed: January 2, 2013

CHAPTER 8
FINANCIAL INFIDELITY

[1]   Allison Linn, *Financial Infidelity Between Couples as Damaging as Sexual Infidelity* http://www.today.com/money/sometimes-we-cheat-our-partners-about-money-survey-shows-731779 (April 24, 2012), Accessed: November 27, 2012.

[2]   Jenna Goudreau, *Is Your Partner Cheating On You Financially? 31% Admit Money Deception* http://www.forbes.com/sites/jennagou-dreau/2011/01/13/is-your-partner-cheating-on-you-financially-31-ad-mit-money-deception-infidelity-red-flags-money-lies/ (January 13, 2011), Accessed: March 11, 2012.

CHAPTER 9
FINANCIAL PORN

[1]   Seth S. Horowitz, "The Science and Art of Listening," *NY Times Sunday Review*, November 9, 2012 (http://www.nytimes.com/2012/11/11/opinion/sunday/why-listening-is-so-much-more-than-hearing.html), Accessed: January 23, 2013.

[2] Bid—an offer made by an investor, a trader, or a dealer to buy a security. The bid will stipulate both the price at which the buyer is willing to purchase the security and the quantity to be purchased.

Ask— the price a seller is willing to accept for a security, also known as the offer price. Along with the price, the ask quote will generally also stipulate the amount of the security willing to be sold at that price.

[3]   Jerry Bowyer, "Let Me Help With The Onrush Of Financial Porn," *Forbes Magazine Online*, March 23, 2011, (http://www.forbes.com/sites/jerrybowyer/2011/03/23/let-me-help-with-the-onrush-of-finan-cial-porn/), Accessed June 4, 2013.

[4]   The term "financial porn" was coined in 1998 by Jane Bryant Quinn. She is an American personal-finance writer who has been teaching and writing on financial wellbeing and disseminating personal finance advice in person, columns, and book.

[5]   Dr. Alvin Cooper was the first to write about the *Triple A engine* effect in 1998.

[6]   Seth Borenstein, "*Sex and financial risk linked in brain,*" Associated Press, http://wwwpsych.stanford.edu/~span/Press/bk040408press.html (April 04, 2008), Accessed: July 6, 2012.

[7]   Robert Weiss, Jennifer P. Schneider, *Closer Together, Further Apart: The Effect of the Internet and Technology on Parenting, Work and Relationships* (Gentle Path Press, 2013)

[8]   Tian Dayton, "Narcissism In A Bottle: The Self-Centeredness Of Addiction," *Huffington Post Online*, Posted 8/2/09, Accessed: August 13, 2013.

CHAPTER 10
MONEY AS AN APHRODISIAC

[1]   Guy Smith, Frontline, "Voices in the Storm: The Brink of War," www.pbs.org/wgbh/pages/frontline/gulf/voices/1.html, Accessed Aug 2, 2013.

[2]   Thomas V. Pollet, Daniel Nettle, "Partner wealth predicts self-reported orgasm frequency in a sample of Chinese women," *Journal of The Human Behavior and Evolution Society*

http://www.ehbonline.org/article/S1090-5138 (08)00117-7/abstract (March 2009), 30:2, 146-151, Accessed: February 15, 2012

[3]   Caroline Waxler, "*Rich Men Give Women More Orgasms,*" http://www.businessinsider.com/2009/1/study-rich-men-give-women-more-orgasms (Jan. 19, 2009), Accessed: July 6, 2012.

[4]   Adrian J. Blow, Kelley Hartnett, "Infidelity in Committed Relationships II: A Substantive Review," *Journal of Marital and Family Therapy,* 31:2 (2005), 217–233 (http://www.jstor.org/), Accessed: September 2, 2102.

[5]   Money and Work Adaptive Styles Index is only administered by clinicians certified by IITAP.

[6]   *Money and Sex,* http://hasaheadache.com/?p=29 (August 27, 2008), Accessed: February 13, 2013.

CHAPTER 11
MONETIZED RAGE

[1]   The Science Show - ABC Radio National, "The Psychopath in Us All," Oct 15, 2011, http://www.abc.net.au/radionational/programs/scienceshow/the-psychopath-in-us-all/3591116#transcript, Accessed: July 7, 2012

[2]   Henry K.S. Nga, Kim-Pong Tamb, Tse-Mei Shu, "The Money Attitude of Covert and Overt Narcissists," *Personality and Individual Differences* 51 (2011) 160–165, (http://www.sciencedirect.com), Accessed: November 4, 2012.

EPILOGUE

[1] Dr. Al Cooper

ABOUT THE AUTHOR

Debra L. Kaplan, MBA, MA, is a licensed therapist in Tucson, Arizona. Her therapy practice specializes in issues of attachment and intimacy, complex traumatic stress and sexual addiction/compulsivity; issues that are often rooted in unresolved childhood trauma. She holds an active faculty position for the International Institute for Trauma and Addiction Professionals (IITAP), and continues to receive training from visionaries in the therapeutic field such as Pia Mellody and Peter Levine. Debra has not forsaken her love of finance and continues to trade her stock and commodity positions.

Made in the USA
Columbia, SC
09 July 2018